Elementary Music Theory

San Marco Publications

Mark Sarnecki

Book 1

Elementary Music Theory © 2023 by San Marco Publications. All rights reserved.

All right reserved. No part of this book may be reproduced in any form or by electronic or mechanical means including Information storage and retrieval systems without permission in writing from the author.

ISNB: 9781896499000

Contents

Johann Sebastian Bach	3
The Keyboard	4
George Frideric Handel	11
The Staff	12
The Treble Clef	15
The Bass Clef	16
Franz Joseph Haydn	18
Notes on the Treble Staff	19
Wolfgang Amadeus Mozart	35
Notes on the Bass Staff	36
Ludwig van Beethoven	52
The Grand Staff	53
Franz Liszt	57
Notes and Time	58
Rests	61

Johann Sebastian Bach
(1685-1750)

Johann Sebastian Bach was born into a musical family in Germany. There were many Bachs who were musicians. He probably had his first music lessons with his father. When he was nine years old, Bach's parents died, and the young musician went to live with his older brother, Christoph. Christoph was a church organist and he taught Johann to play the organ and harpsichord.

Bach began his career as a court musician. In 1723 he moved to Leipzig, where he became music director for the city. He wrote several hundred pieces for keyboard instruments. He also composed many cantatas for church services, as well as orchestral pieces and concertos.

Bach was one of the great teachers of his time. He taught music to his children. Four of them became well known composers. He had many other pupils over the years. Some of his students lived in his household and helped him with musical tasks. Much of Bach's keyboard music was written for teaching.

The Keyboard

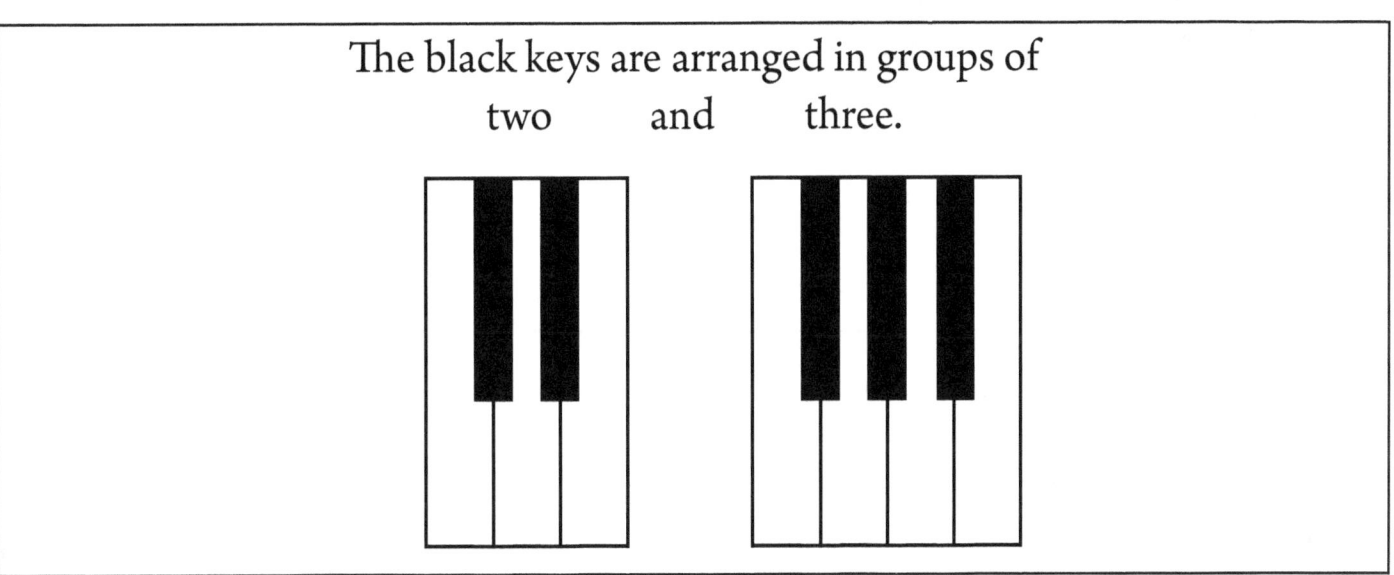

The black keys are arranged in groups of two and three.

1. Circle all the groups of two black keys

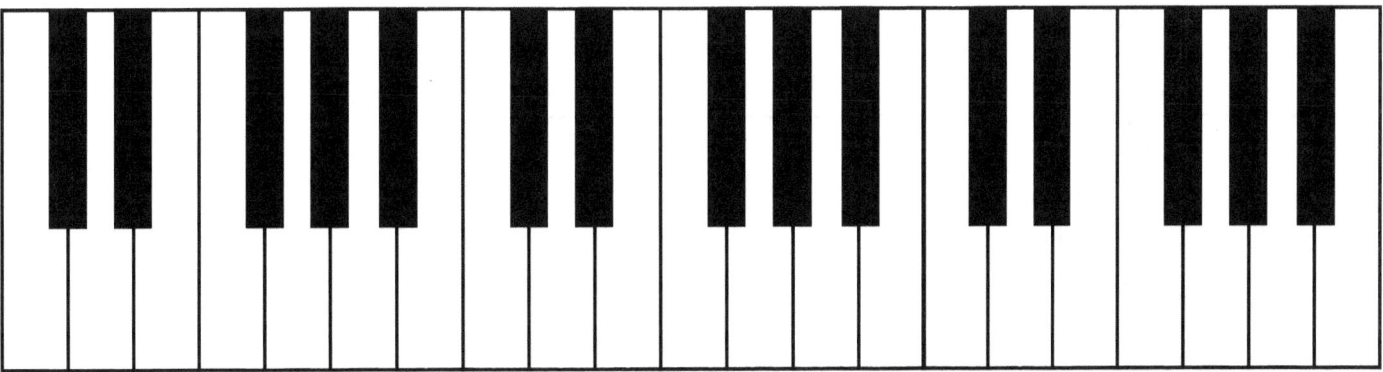

2. Circle all the groups of three black keys

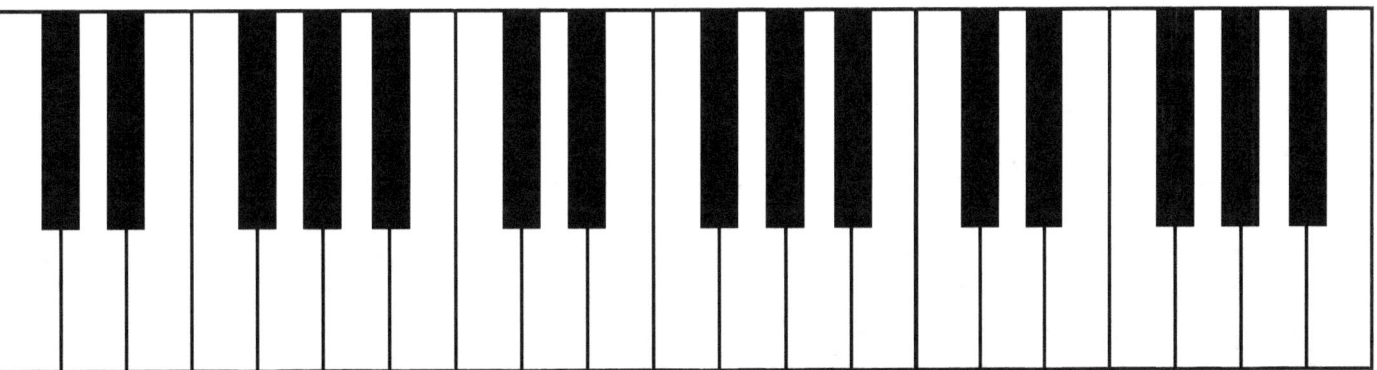

The Musical Alphabet consists of seven letters:
A B C D E F G

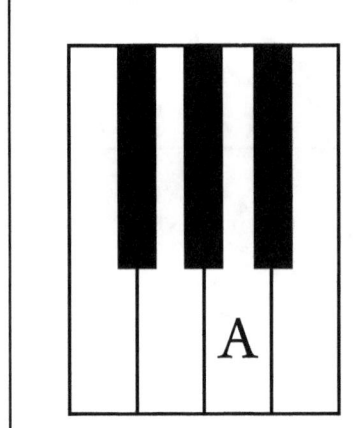  is found between the second and third keys of any group of three black keys.

3. Find all the As on this keyboard. Print A on each one.

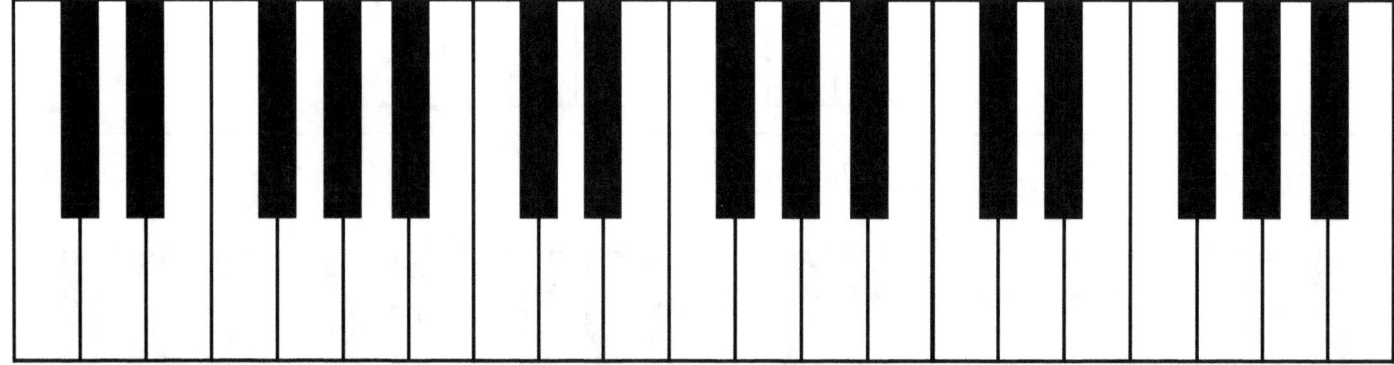

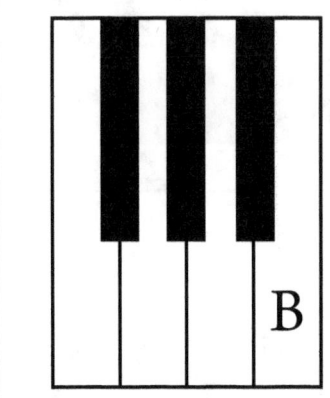  is found on the right side of any group of three black keys.

4. Find all the Bs on this keyboard. Print B on each one.

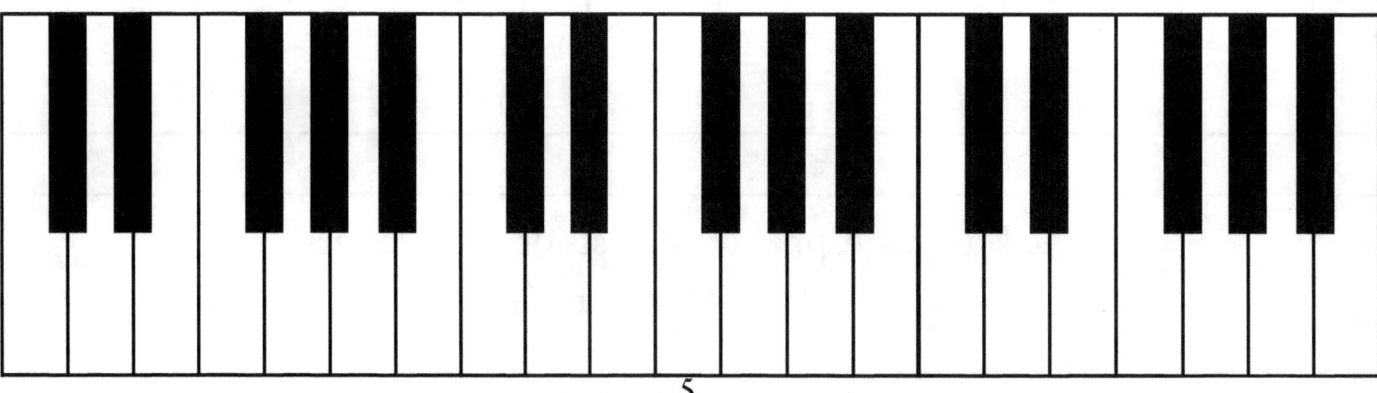

5

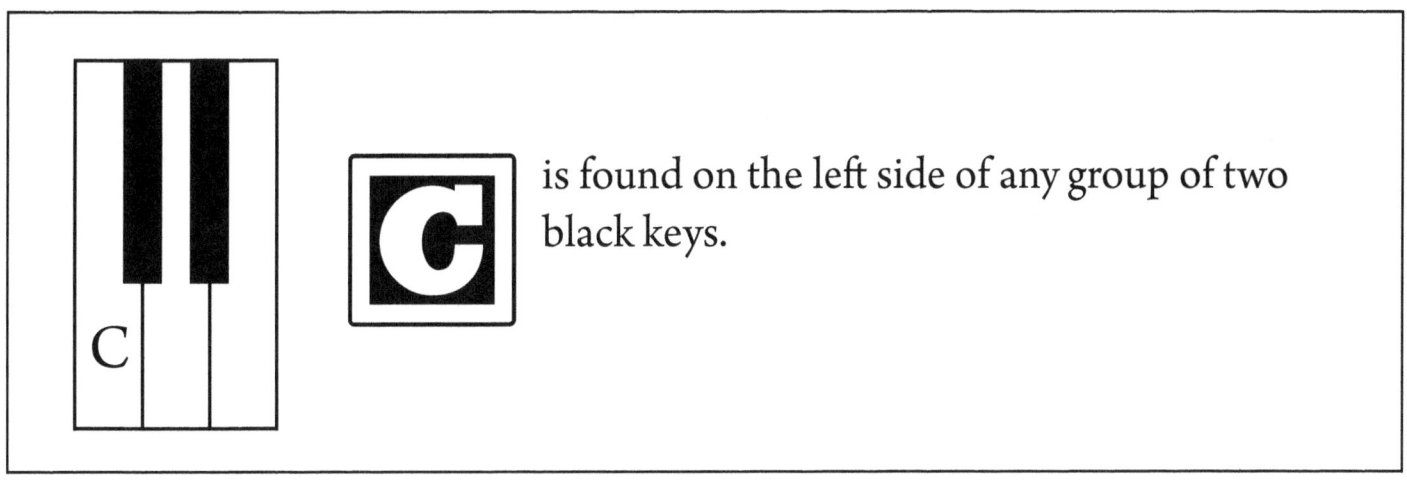

C is found on the left side of any group of two black keys.

5. Find all the Cs on this keyboard. Print C on each one.

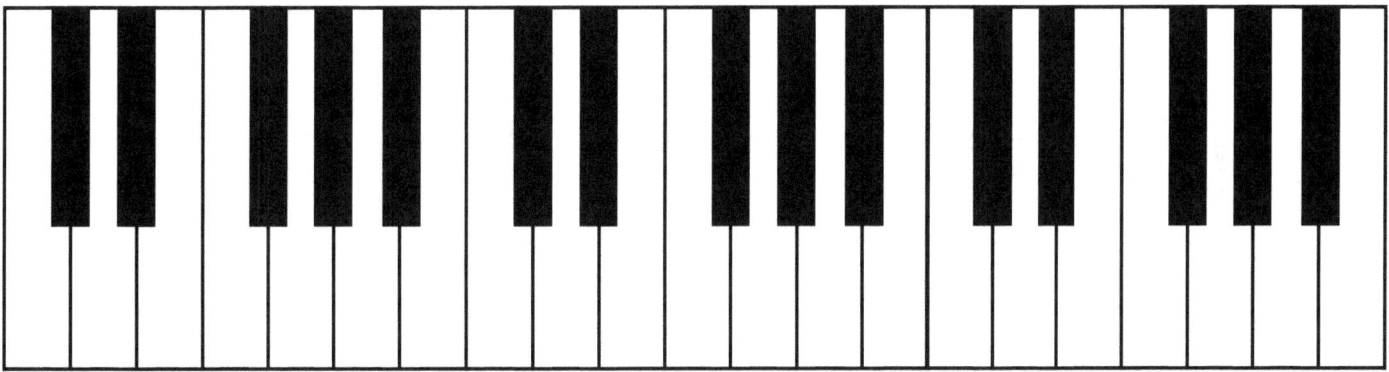

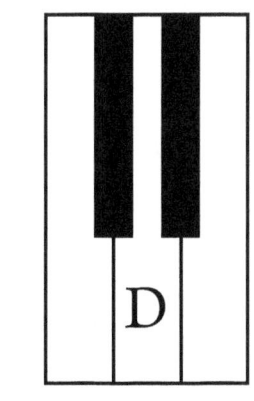

D is found in the middle of any group of two black keys.

6. Find all the Ds on this keyboard. Print D on each one.

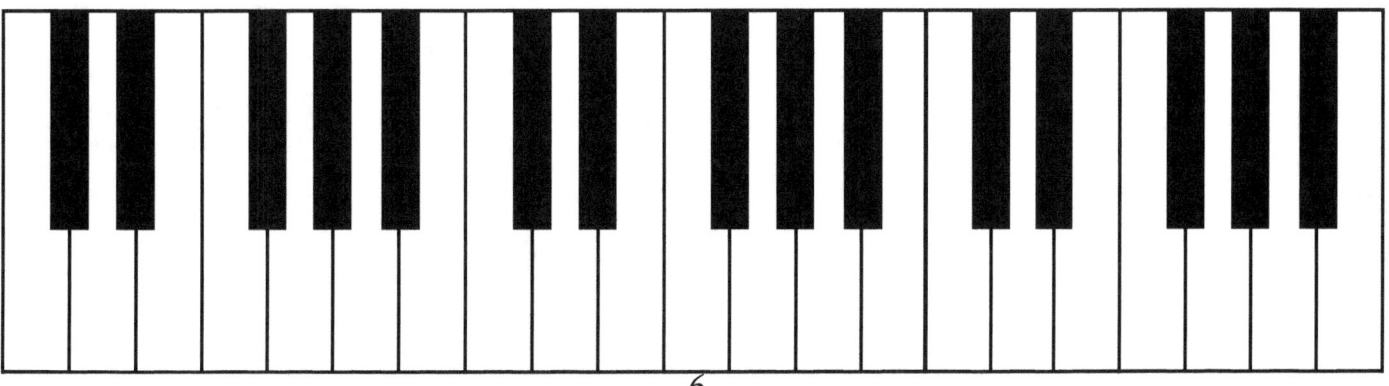

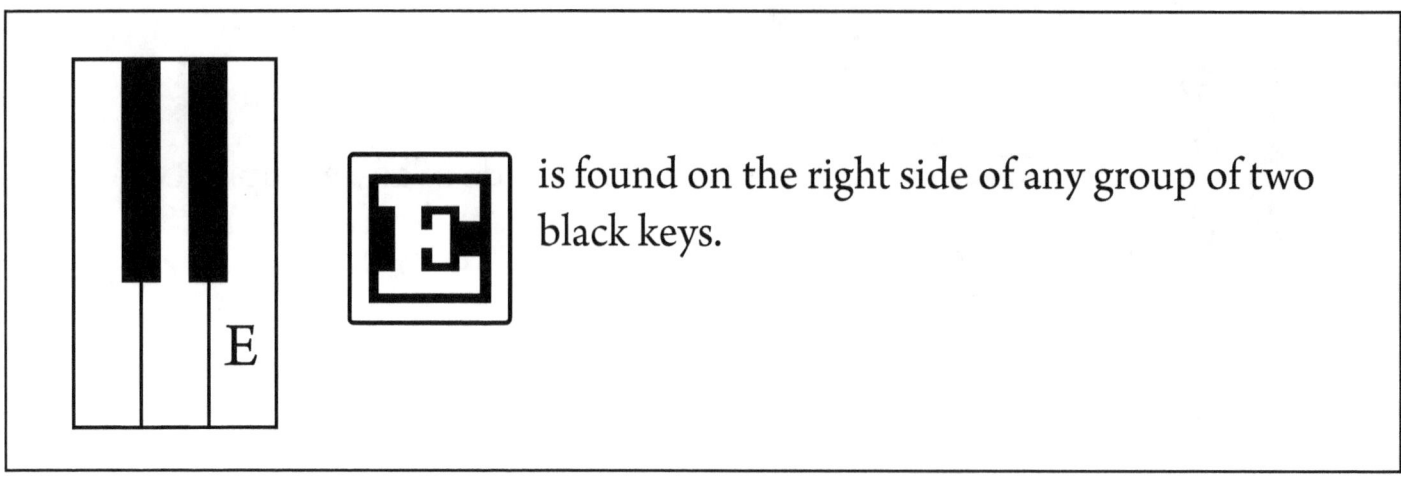

E is found on the right side of any group of two black keys.

7. Find all the Es on this keyboard. Print E on each one.

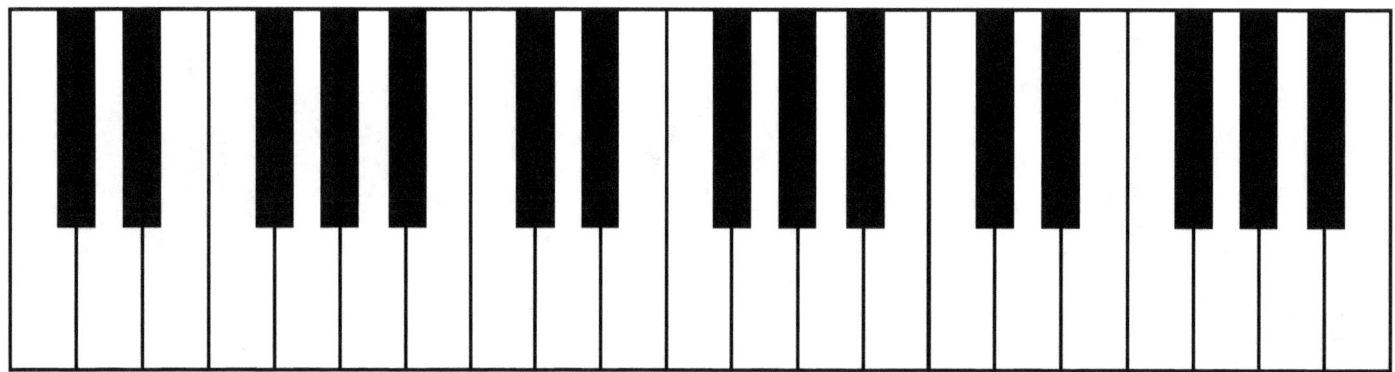

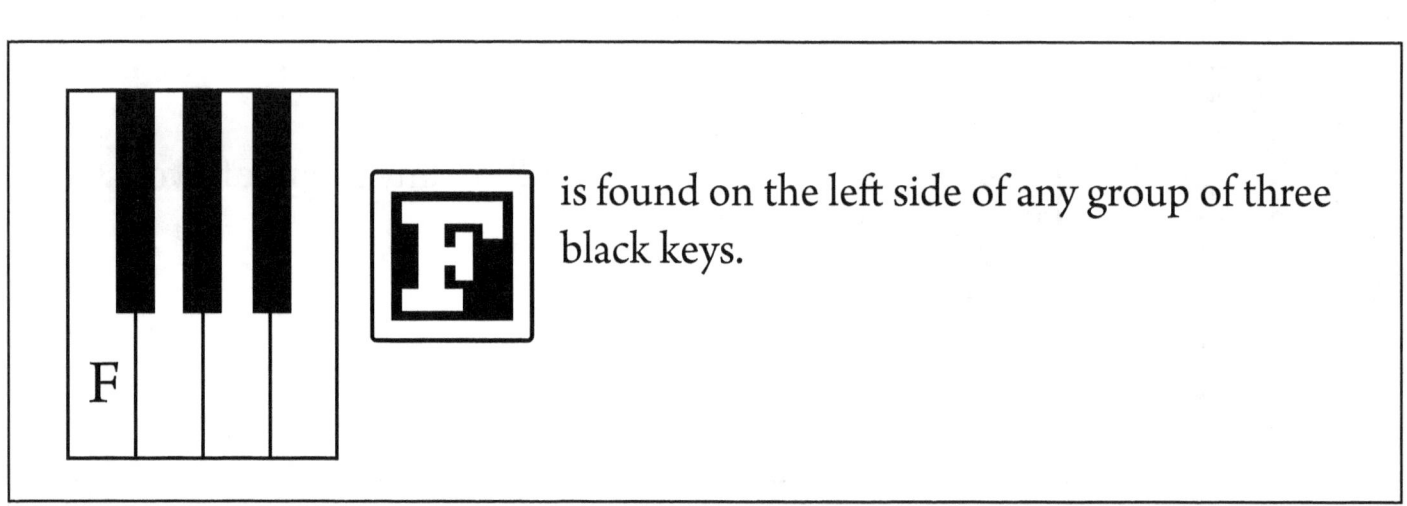

F is found on the left side of any group of three black keys.

8. Find all the Fs on this keyboard. Print F on each one.

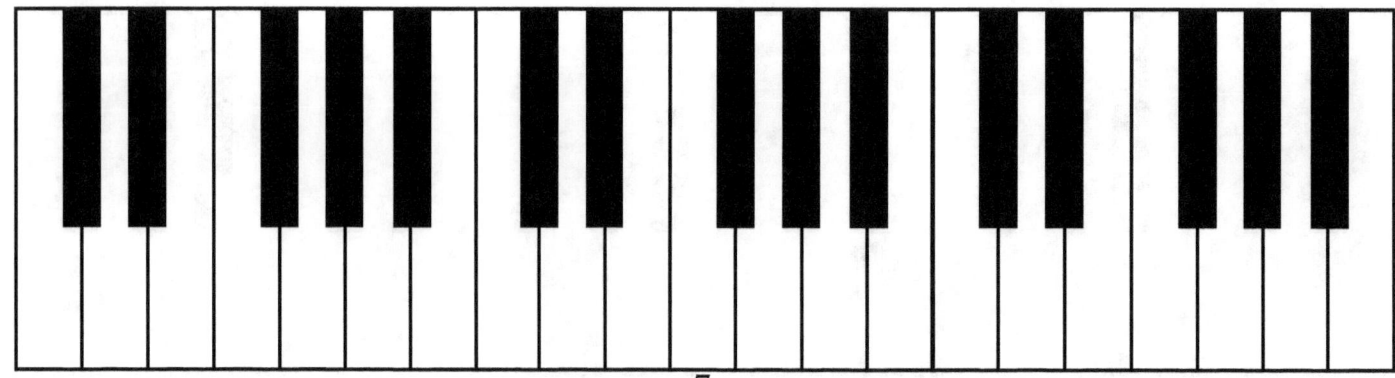

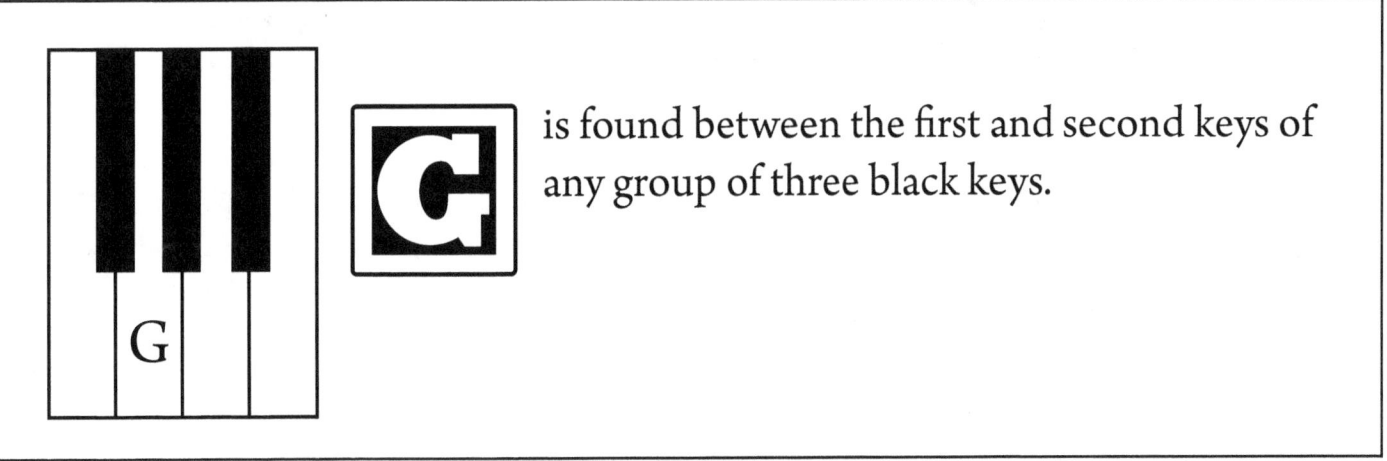

G is found between the first and second keys of any group of three black keys.

9. Find all the Gs on this keyboard. Print G on each one.

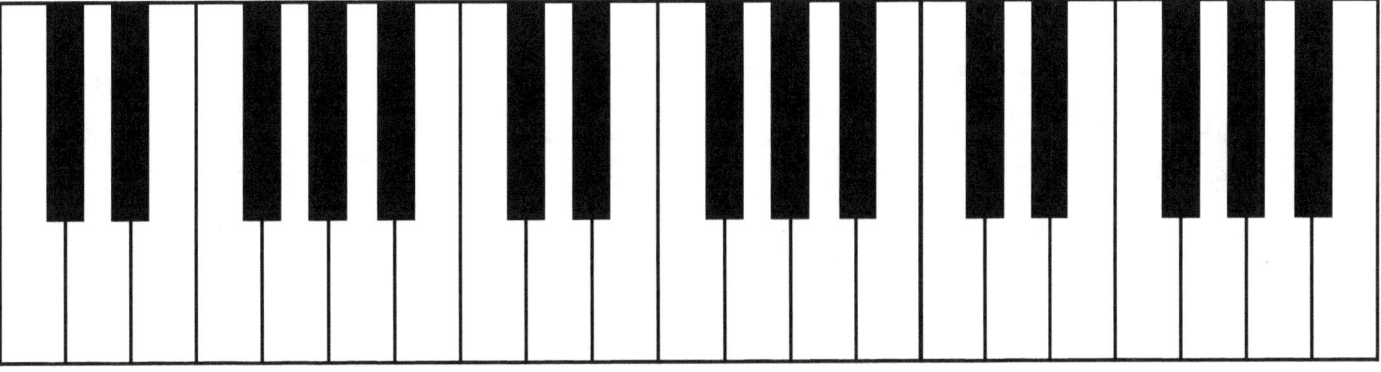

10. On the keyboard below, print the names of all the keys.

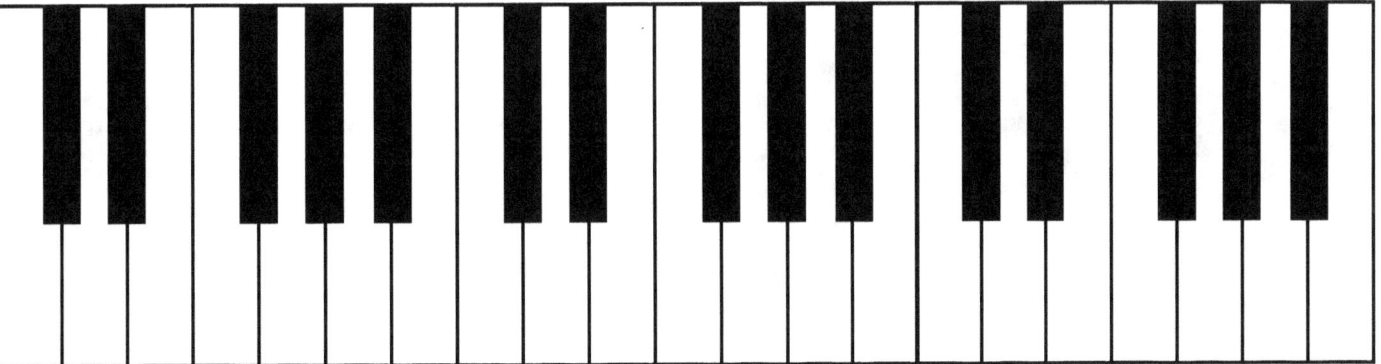

Good work!
You know the keyboard!

SPELLING FUN

1. Name the keys marked with stars to find words.

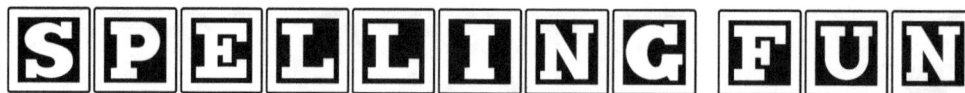

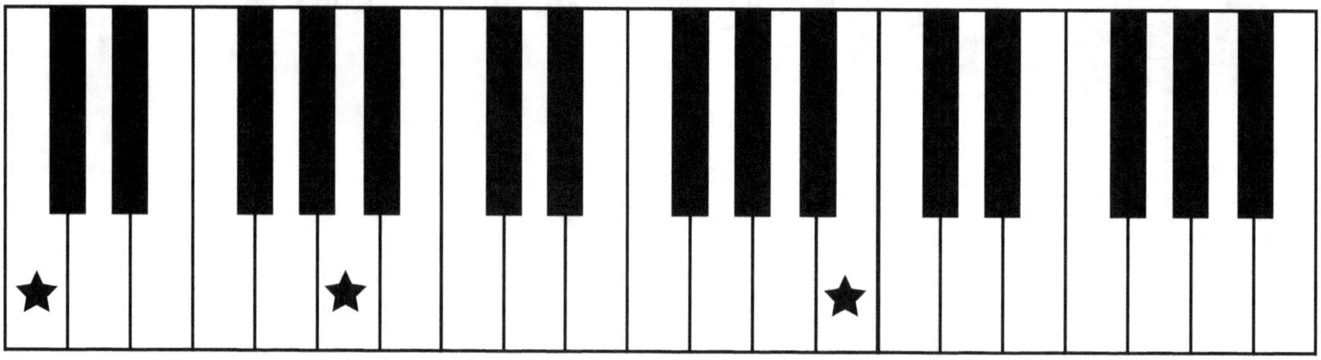

C A

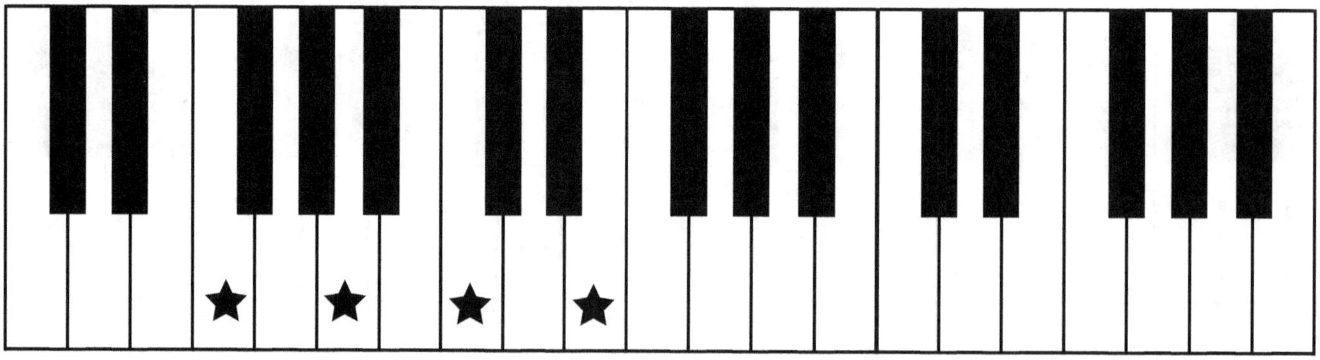

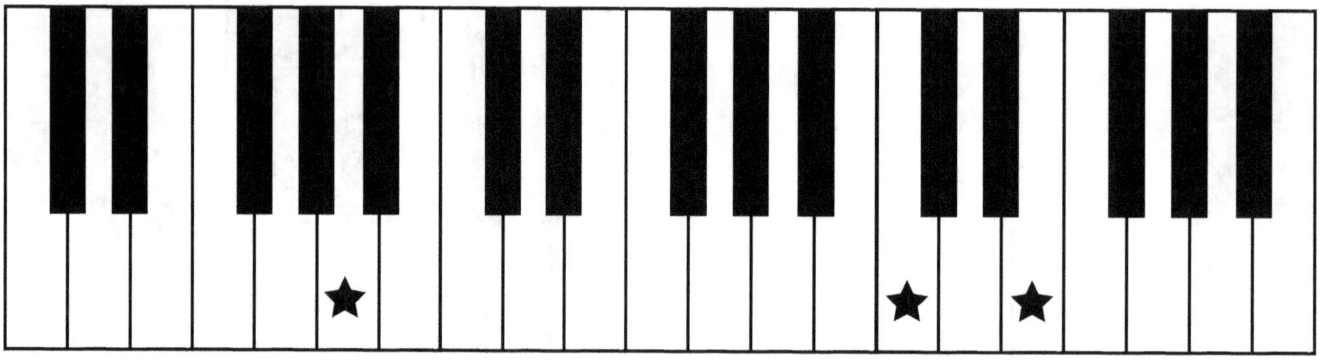

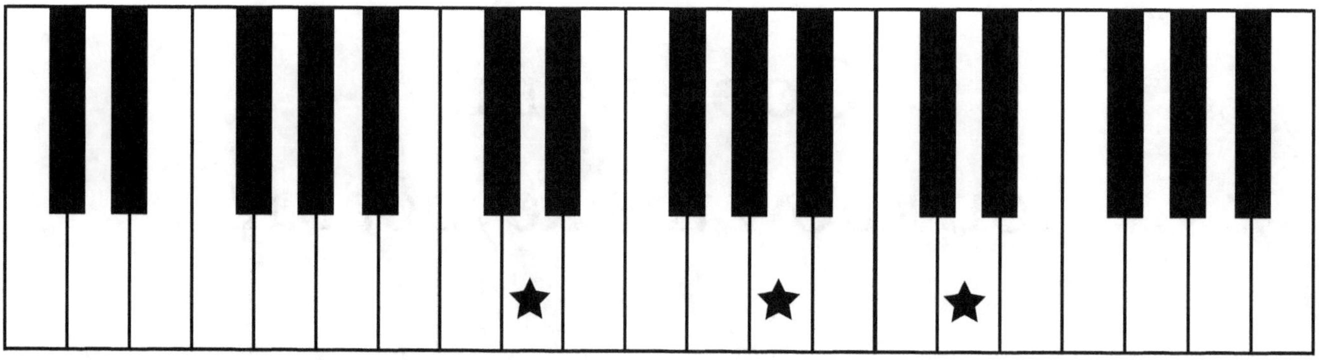

2. Write the following words on the keyboards below.

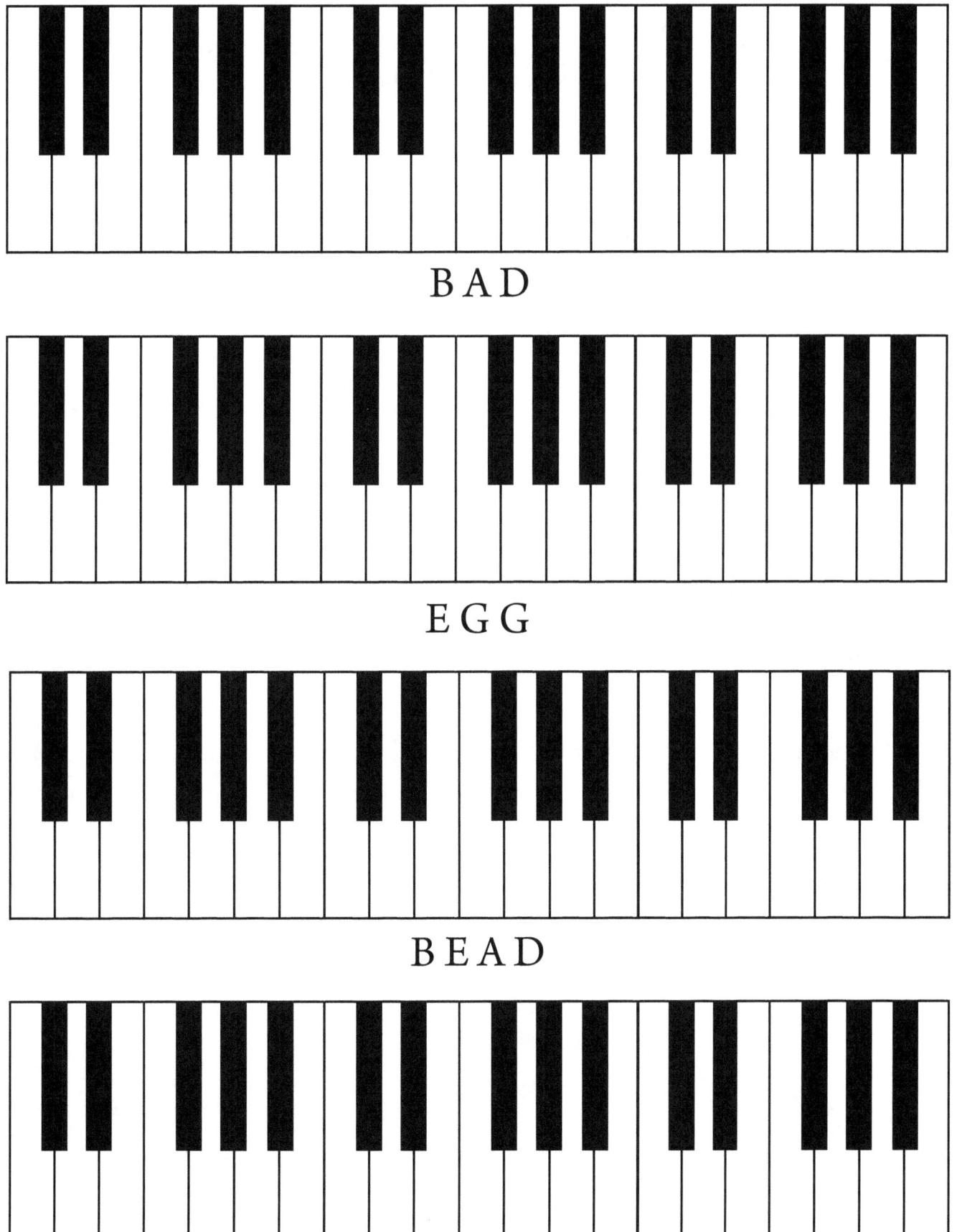

George Frideric Handel
(1685-1759)

Handel was born in Germany. He wanted to become a musician but he was not allowed to practice at home. However, at age eleven, Handel could play four instruments: harpsichord, organ, violin and oboe.

When he was about twenty-seven years old, Handel went to England. He composed operas, hired a theater, paid the singers, sold the tickets, and led the performances. He made and lost huge sums of money. He also wrote a ton of music.

Handel spent the rest of his life in England. He became a particular favorite of the royal court. He taught keyboard to the daughters of King George II. He was one of the most popular composers of his time. His orchestral music and some of his oratorios are still very popular today.

The Staff

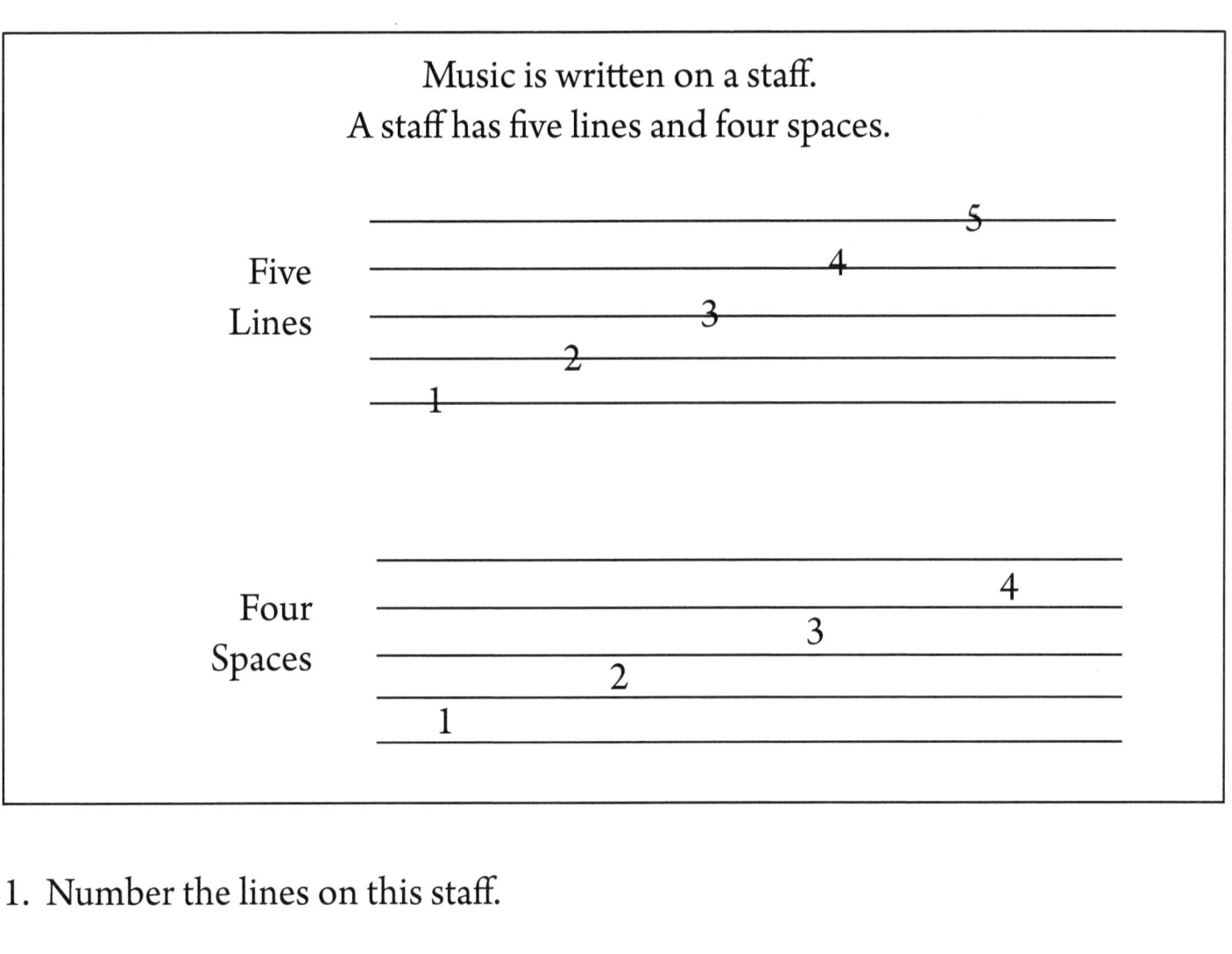

1. Number the lines on this staff.

2. Number the spaces on this staff.

Musical notes are written **on** the five lines

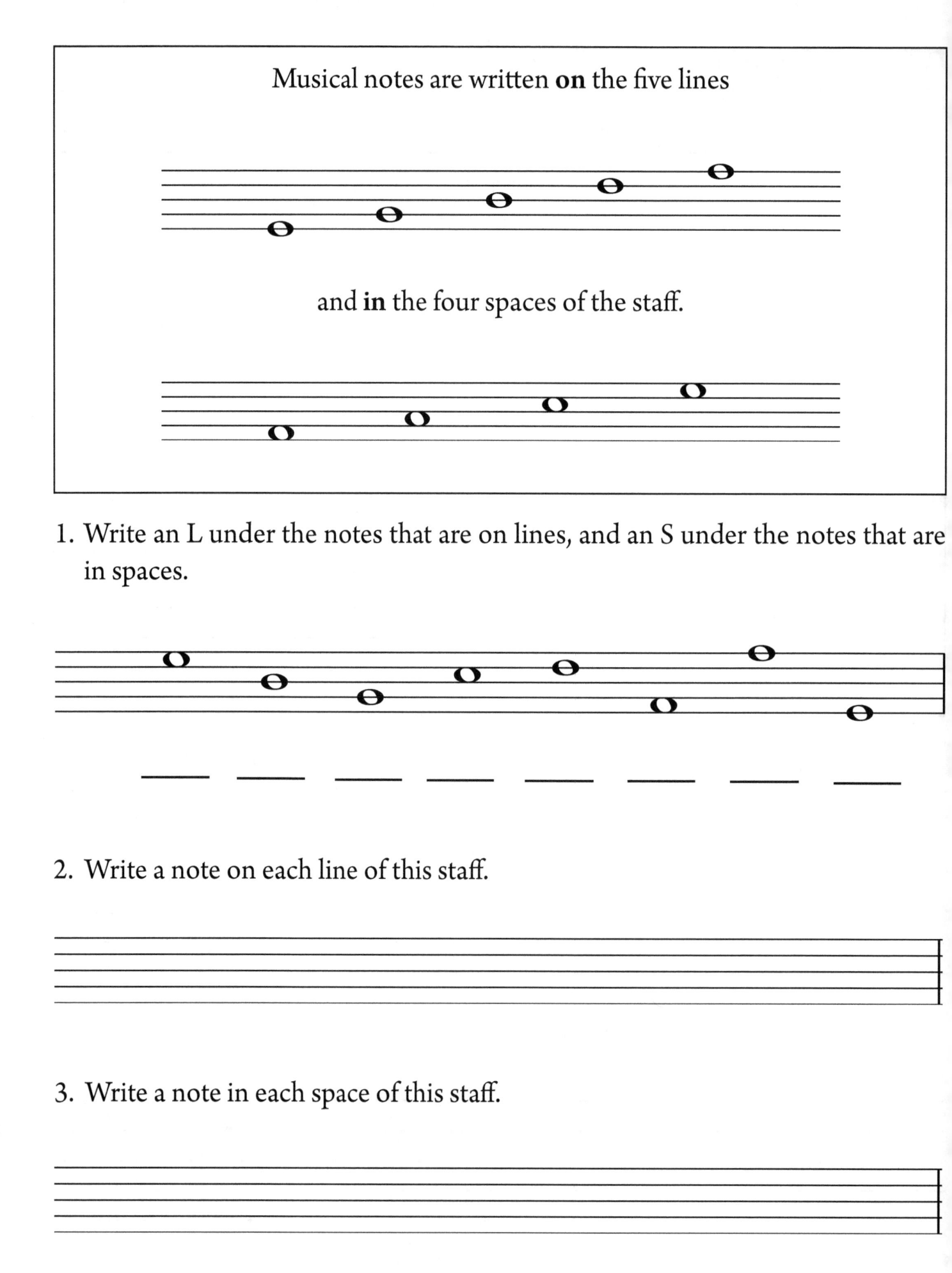

and **in** the four spaces of the staff.

1. Write an L under the notes that are on lines, and an S under the notes that are in spaces.

2. Write a note on each line of this staff.

3. Write a note in each space of this staff.

4. Write notes on these line numbers.

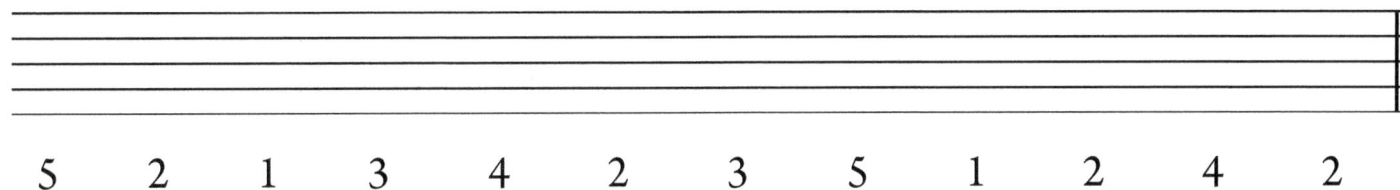

5 2 1 3 4 2 3 5 1 2 4 2

5. Write notes on these space numbers.

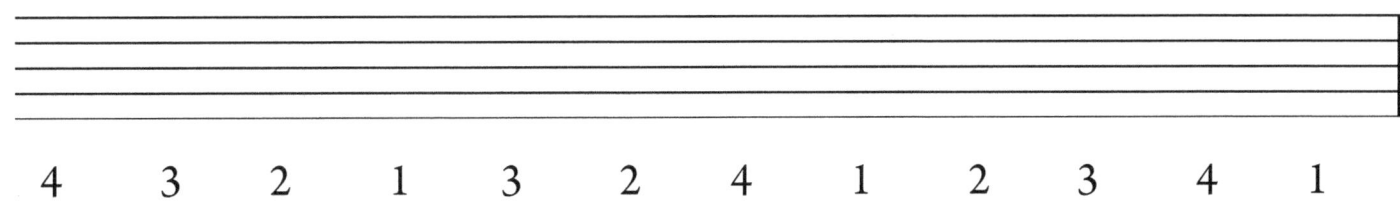

4 3 2 1 3 2 4 1 2 3 4 1

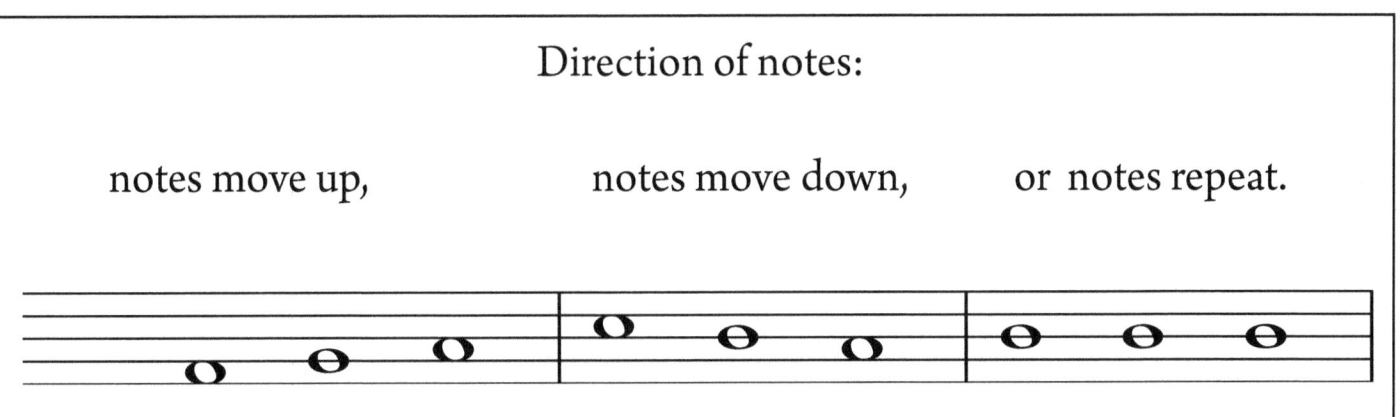

Direction of notes:

notes move up,   notes move down,   or notes repeat.

6. Circle the answer that shows the direction of these notes.

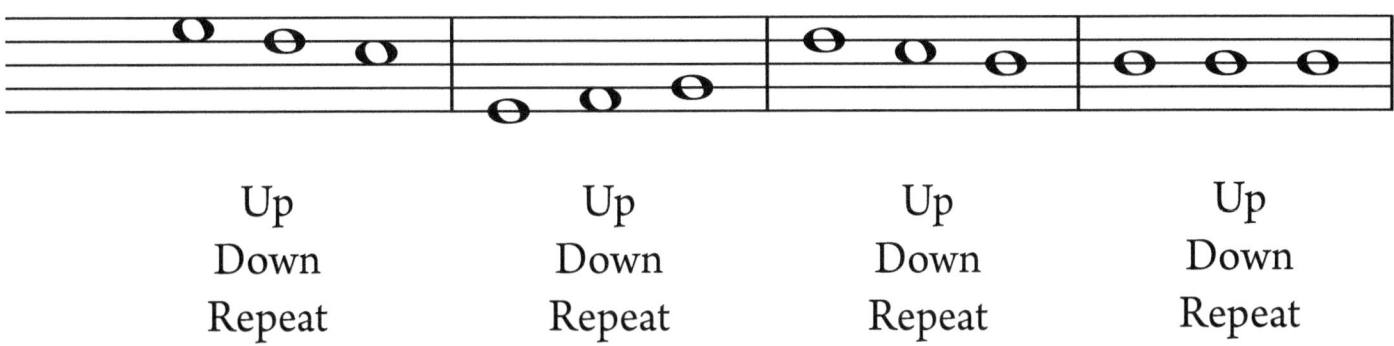

    Up   Up   Up   Up
Down   Down   Down   Down
Repeat   Repeat   Repeat   Repeat

The Treble Clef

Clefs tell us which notes are on each line and space.
Higher notes in music are written in the treble clef.
The right hand usually plays in the treble clef.
The treble clef is found at the beginning of the staff.

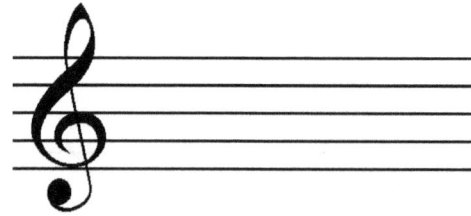

It's easy to draw a treble clef!

1. Practice drawing treble clefs by tracing the ones below.

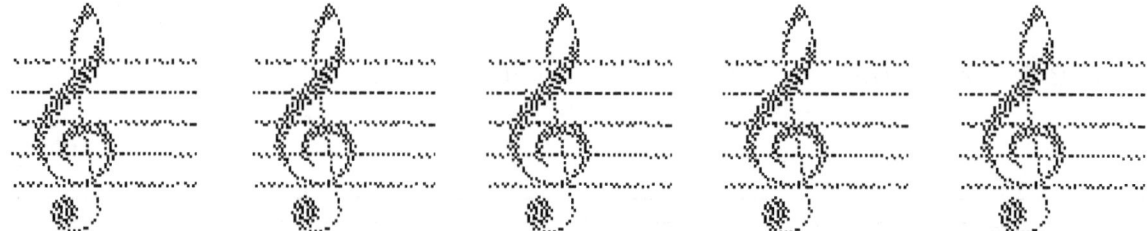

2. Draw five treble clefs on the staff below.

The Bass Clef

Lower notes in music are written in the bass clef.
The left hand usually plays in the bass clef.
The bass clef is found at the beginning of the staff.

It's easy to draw a bass clef!

1. 2. 3.

1. Practice drawing bass clefs by tracing the ones below.

2. Draw five bass clefs on the staff below.

MATCHING FUN

Draw lines matching these symbols with their names.

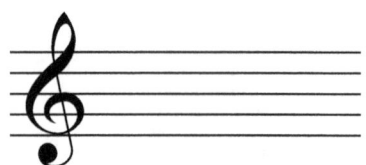

group of two black keys

treble clef

notes in spaces

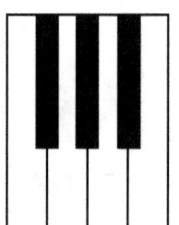

group of three black keys

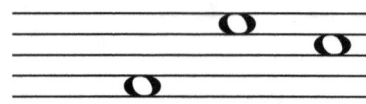

bass clef

notes on lines

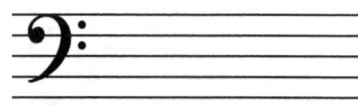

notes moving up

notes moving down

Franz Joseph Haydn
(1732-1809)

Haydn was born in a small Austrian village near the Hungarian border. His father, Mathias Haydn, made and repaired wheels. His mother, Maria Anna, was a cook. As a child Haydn would have heard many peasant folk songs.

Haydn began his musical life as a choirboy in Vienna. When he left the choir school at age seventeen, he was poor and homeless, but his musical talents brought him to the notice of wealthy nobility. He spent thirty years as music director for the Esterhazy family of Hungary. A small resident orchestra played Haydn's chamber music, concertos, and symphonies.

When Haydn came back to Vienna in 1790, his fame had spread across Europe. Haydn was a likable person. He was kind and generous to his fellow musicians, including Mozart, whom he met in 1781. His music reflects his pleasant character... it is cheerful and full of good humor.

Notes on the Treble Staff

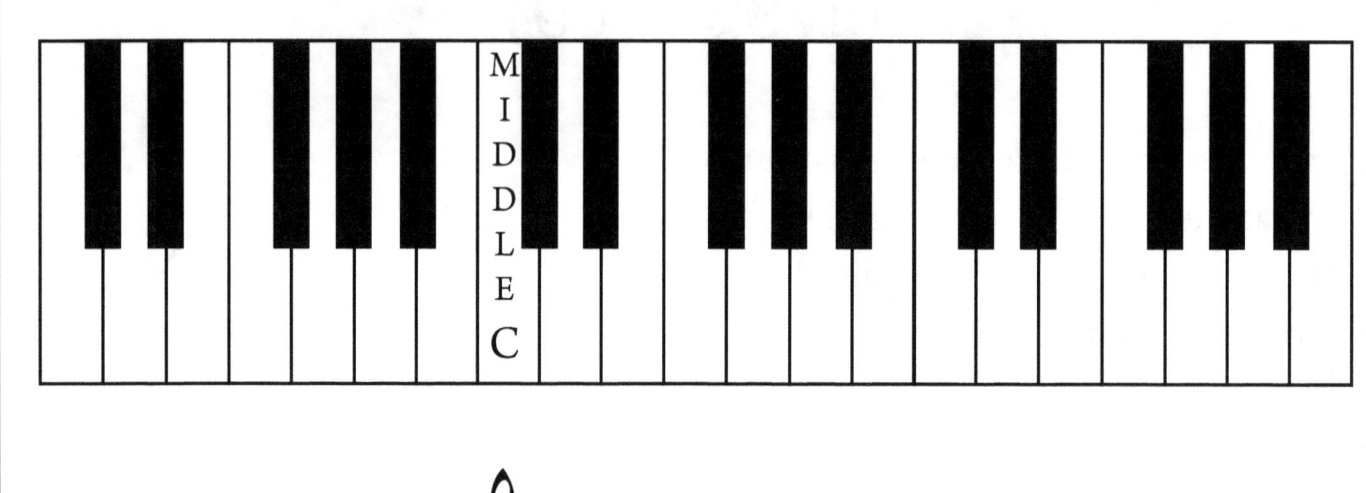

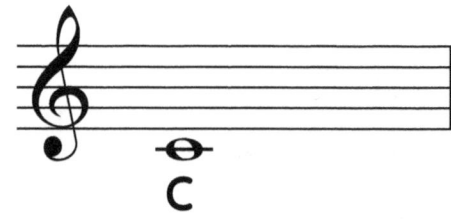

Middle C is found below the treble staff. It has its own line.
This line is called a ledger line.

1. Draw a treble clef at the beginning of each staff. Write two lines of middle Cs.

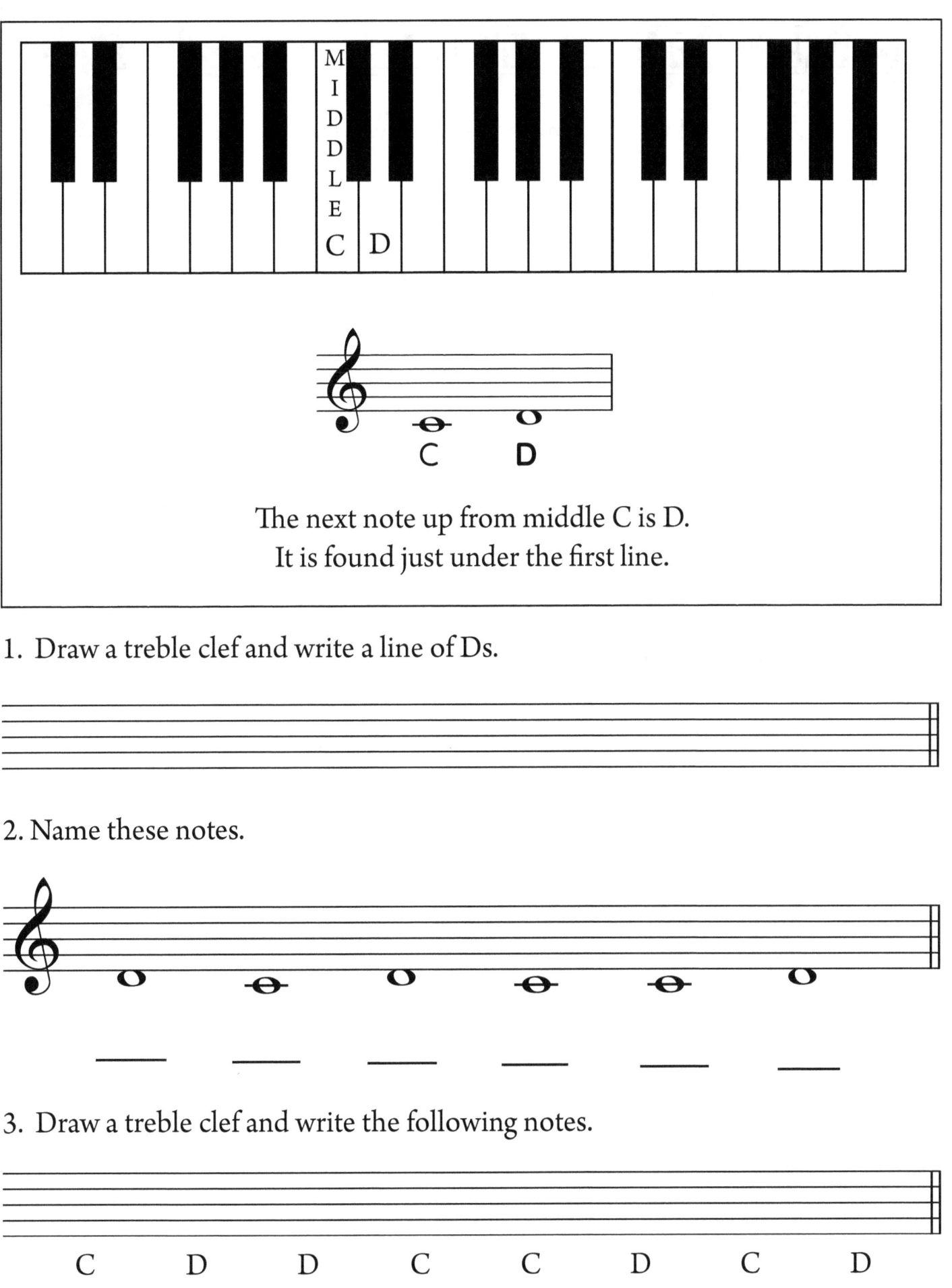

The next note up from middle C is D.
It is found just under the first line.

1. Draw a treble clef and write a line of Ds.

2. Name these notes.

3. Draw a treble clef and write the following notes.

C D D C C D C D

MUSICAL WORD PUZZLE

Find words from the list below in this puzzle.

```
J T H R E E E H K H N
S R N P D K T E F R
Q E W M O E S Y O E
S B L I W Y P B U P
T L I D N U A O R E
A E N D W P C A B A
F S E L C H E R A T
F I V E L L I D S T
I S U C N D E T S W
Q V B L A C K F E O
```

√key   five
keyboard   four
black   up
white   down
two   repeat
three   clef
staff   bass
line   treble
space   middle C

21

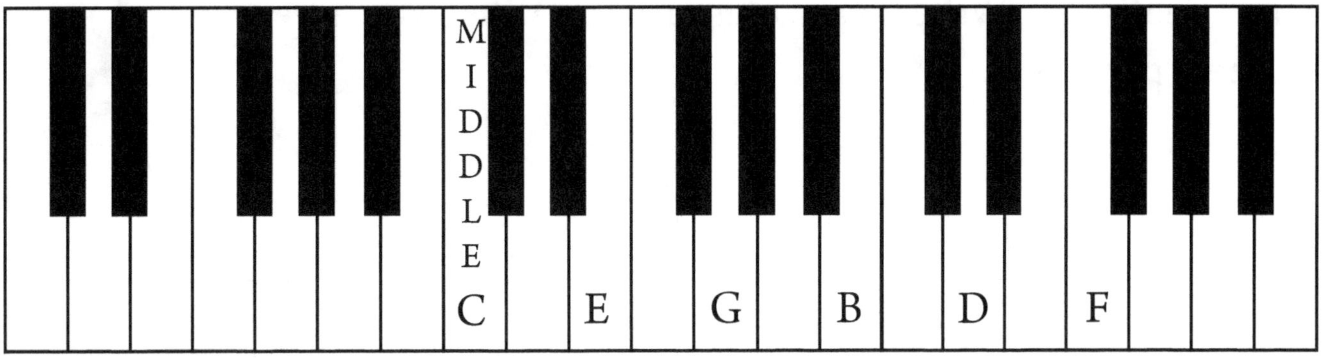

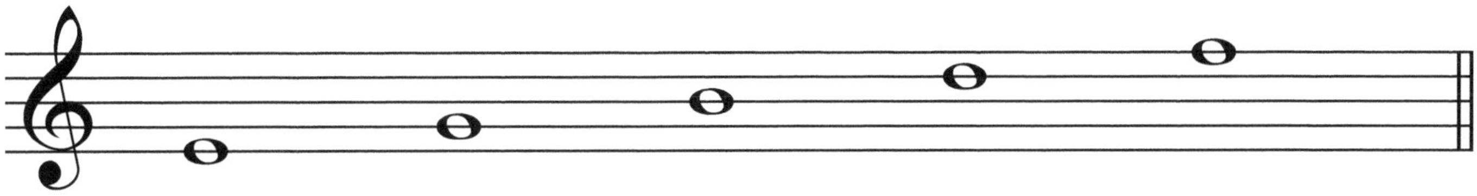

Here are the notes on the five lines of the treble staff:

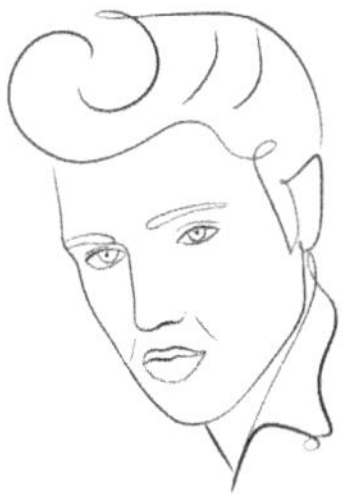

E G B D F

Elvis' **G**uitar **B**roke **D**own **F**riday

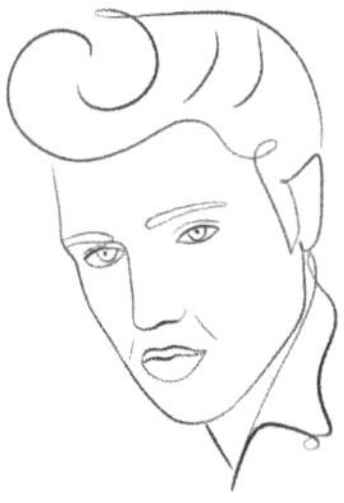

1. Name these notes. When you have finished, play them!

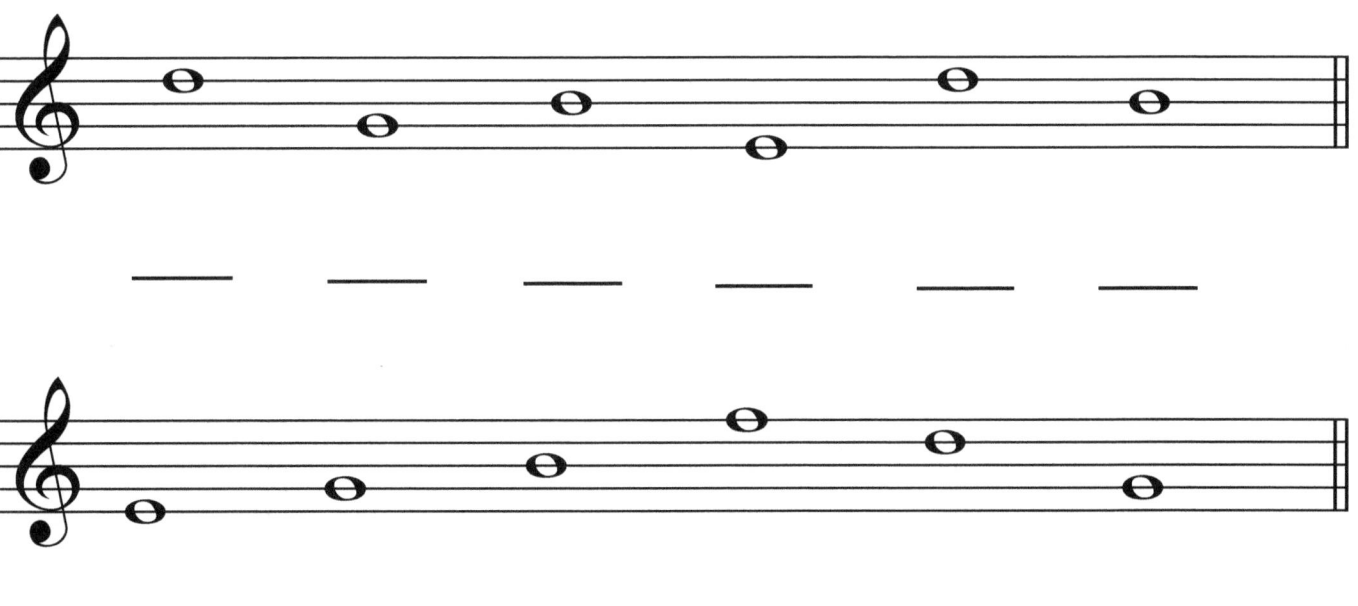

2. Draw treble clefs. Write these notes on lines. When you have finished, play them!

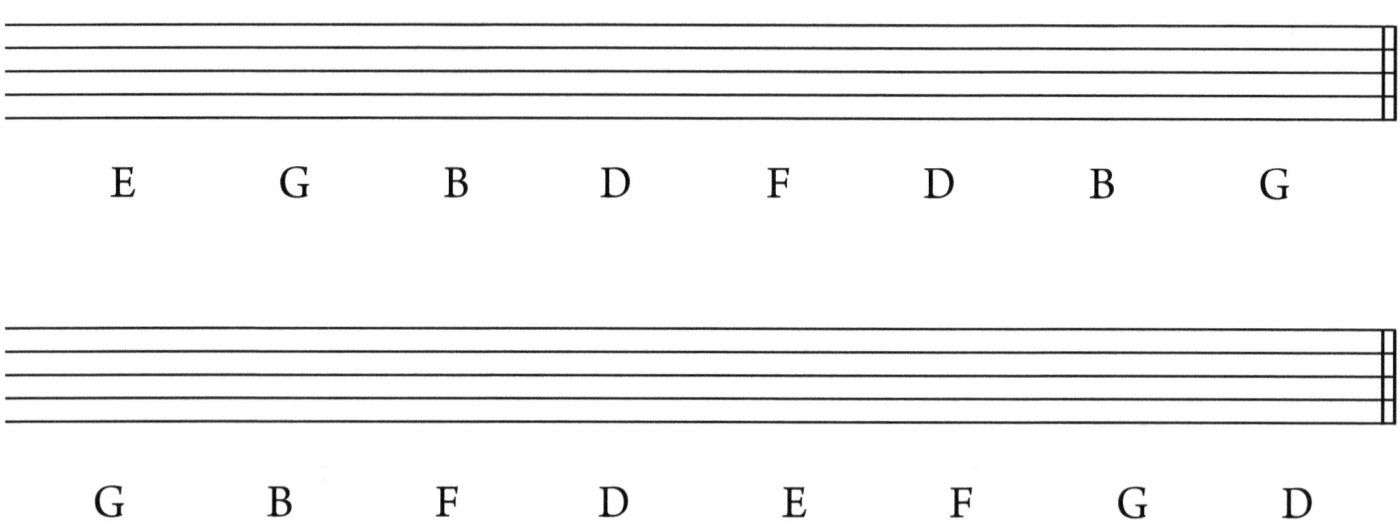

E   G   B   D   F   D   B   G

G   B   F   D   E   F   G   D

3. Name these notes.

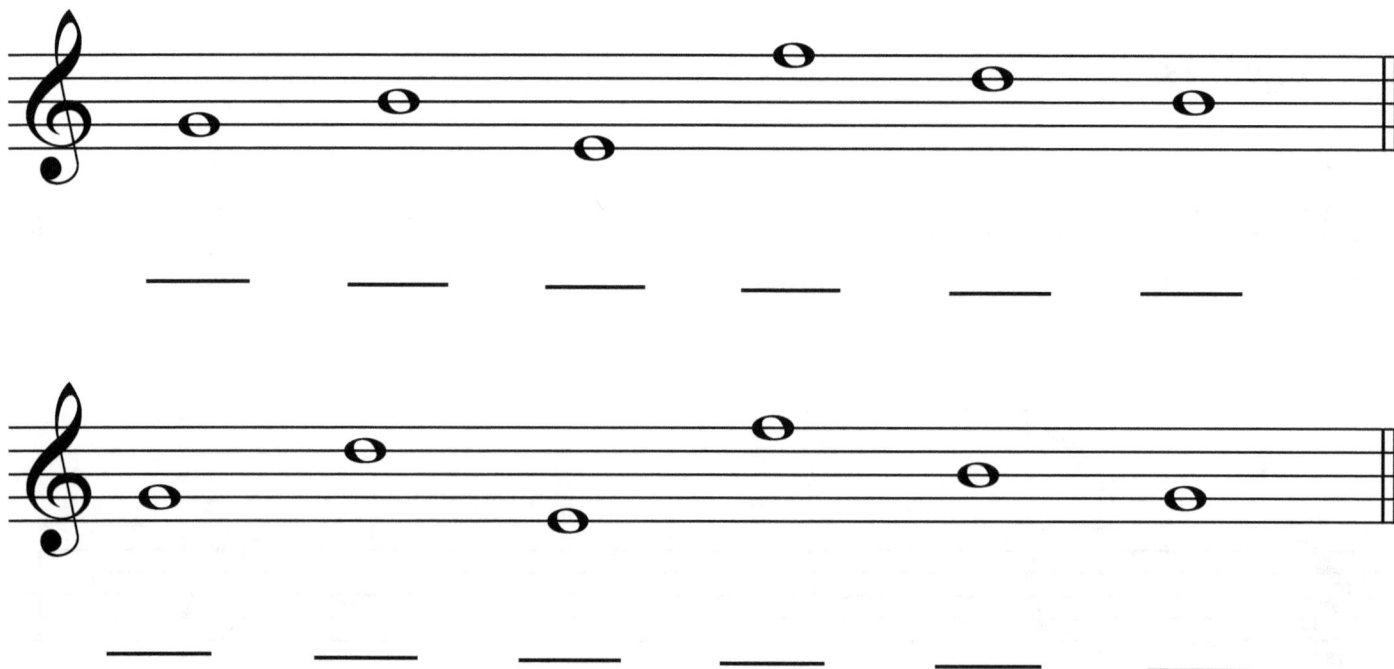

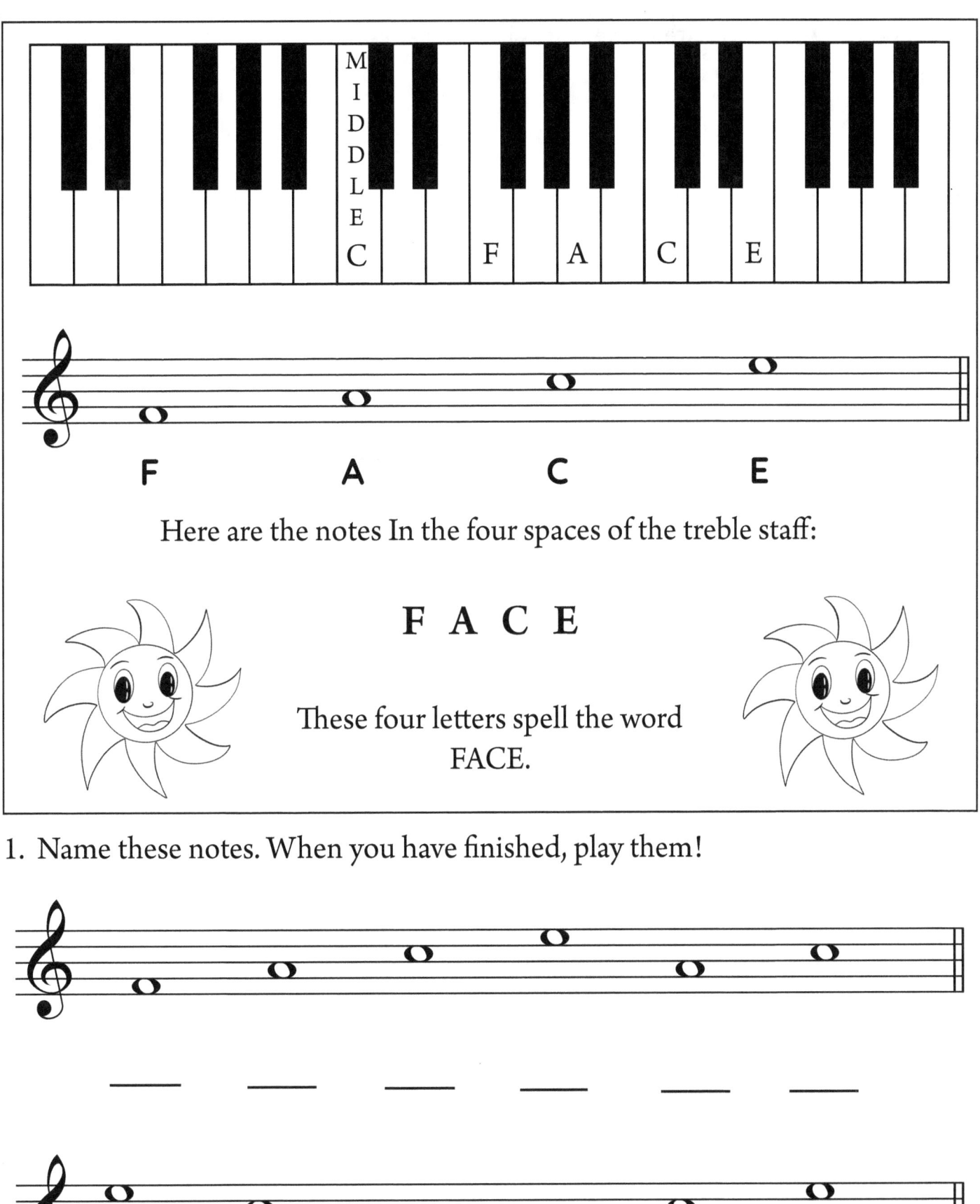

Here are the notes In the four spaces of the treble staff:

F A C E

These four letters spell the word FACE.

1. Name these notes. When you have finished, play them!

2. Draw treble clefs. Write these notes in spaces. When you have finished, play them!

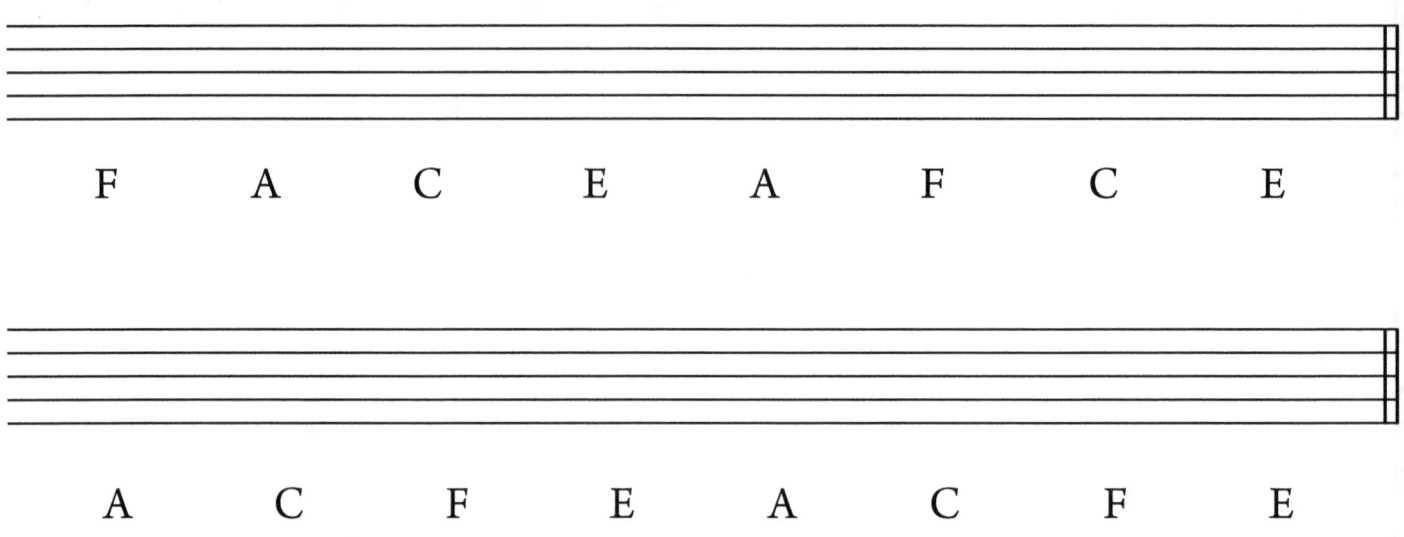

3. Name these notes.

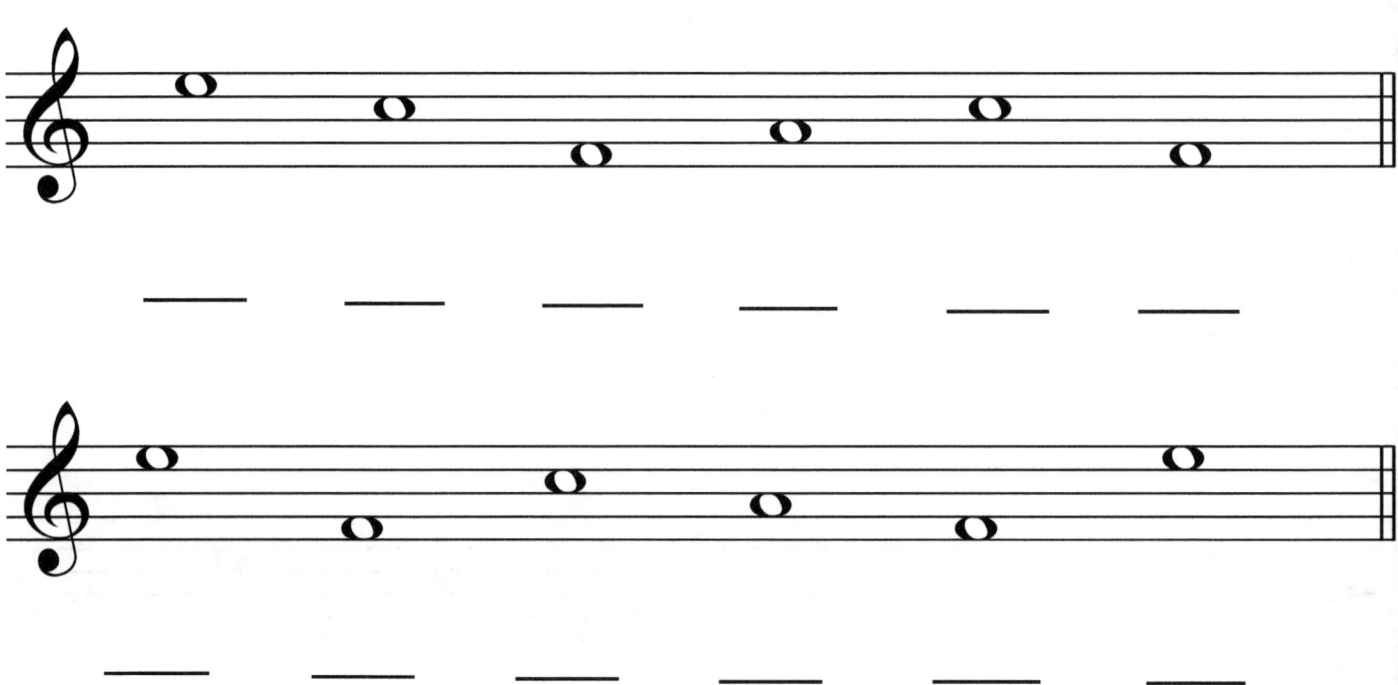

You have learned most of the notes on the treble staff.
Let's practice writing them!

4. Write these notes in the treble staff. Use both lines and spaces. When you have finished, play them.

G   D   B   A   C   F   middleC   E

F   B   E   D   C   A   G   D

middle C   G   B   D   A   E   F   C

G   B   D   E   A   D   C   F

Did you remember to draw treble clefs?

5. Name these notes.

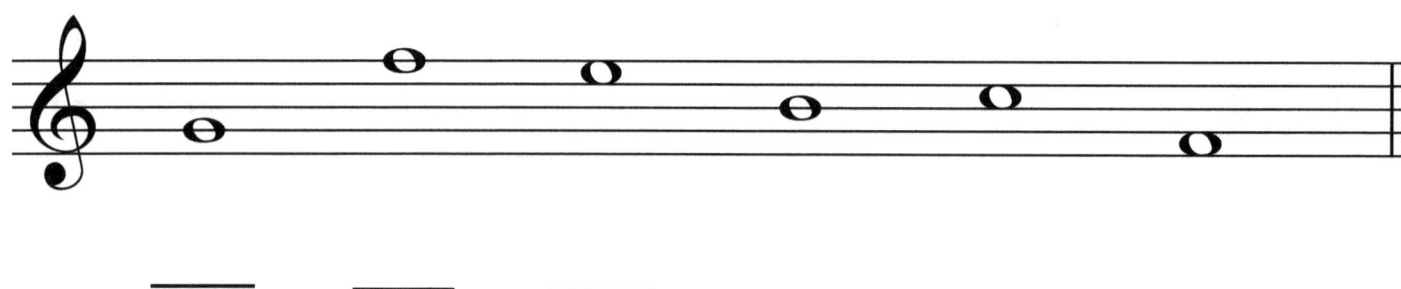

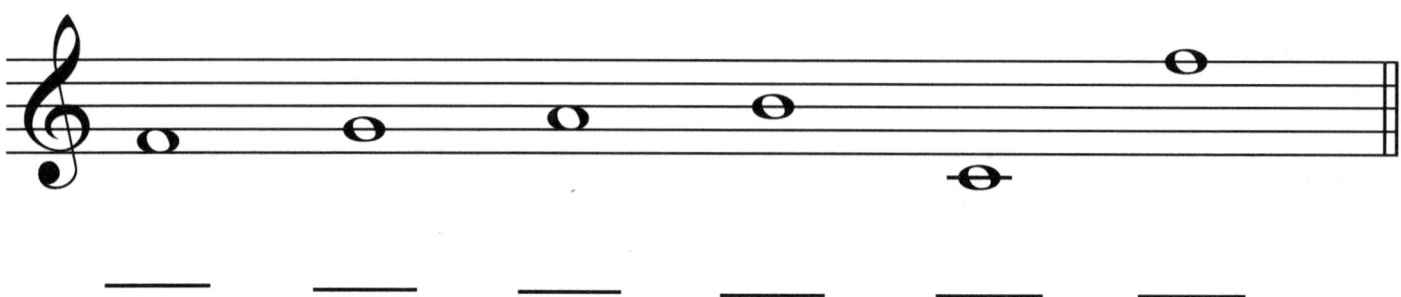

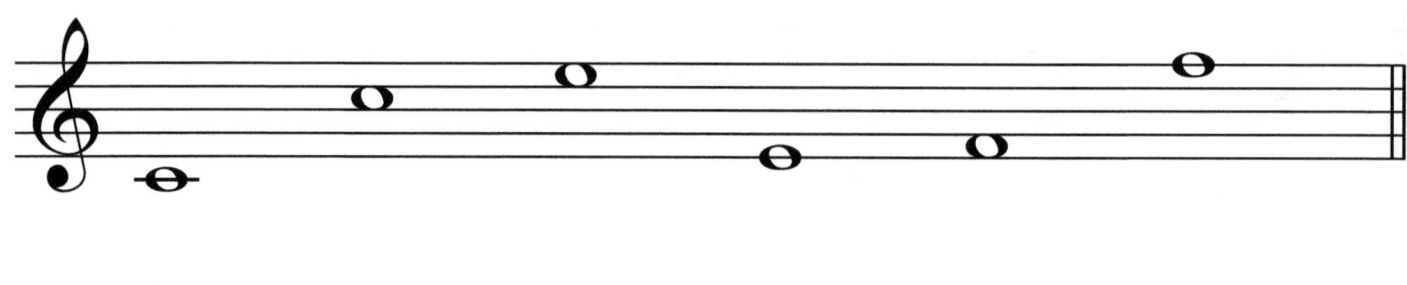

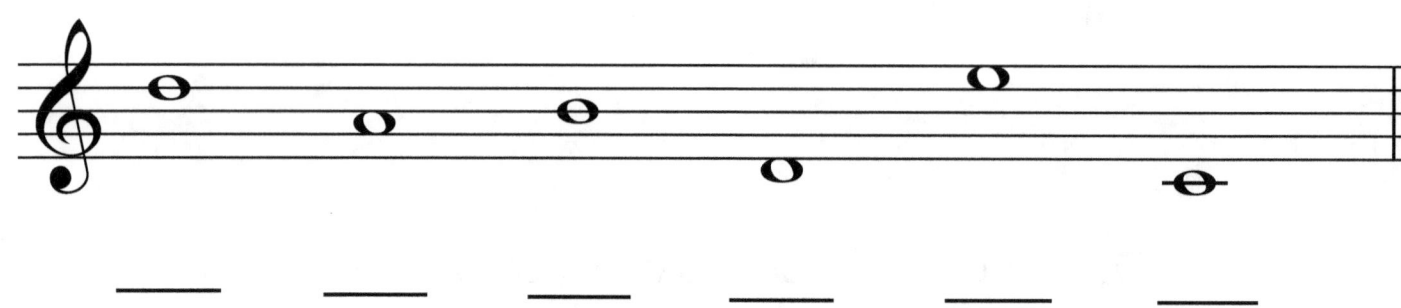

6. Beginning with middle C, write all the treble clef notes ascending.
   Write the letter name under each note.

7. Beginning with high F (line 5), write all the treble clef notes descending.
   Write the letter name under each note.

Musical Signs

p	piano	soft
mp	mezzo piano	moderately soft
f	forte	loud
mf	mezzo forte	moderately loud
rit.	ritardando	slowing down gradually
	double bar	the end of a section
		the end of the music

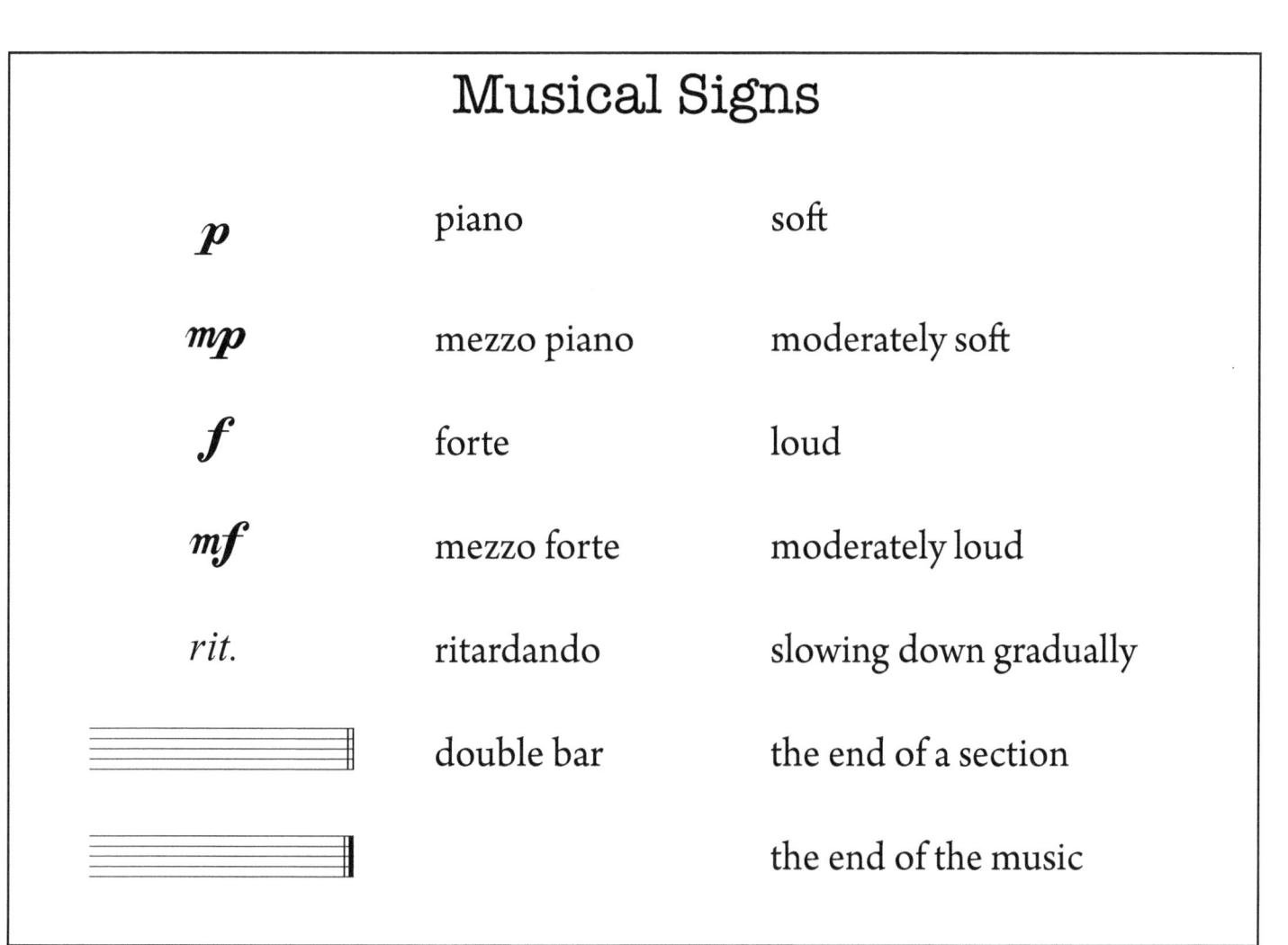

8. Name these notes. Draw lines connecting them to the keys on the keyboards.

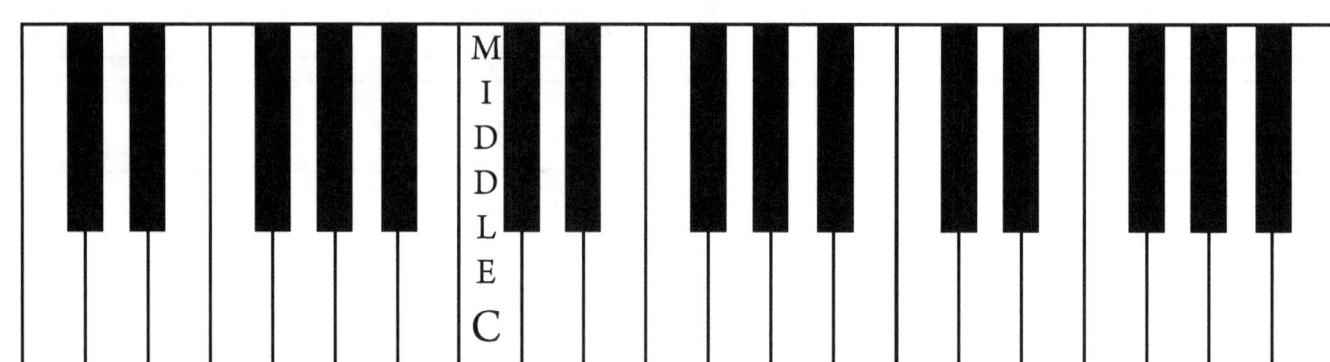

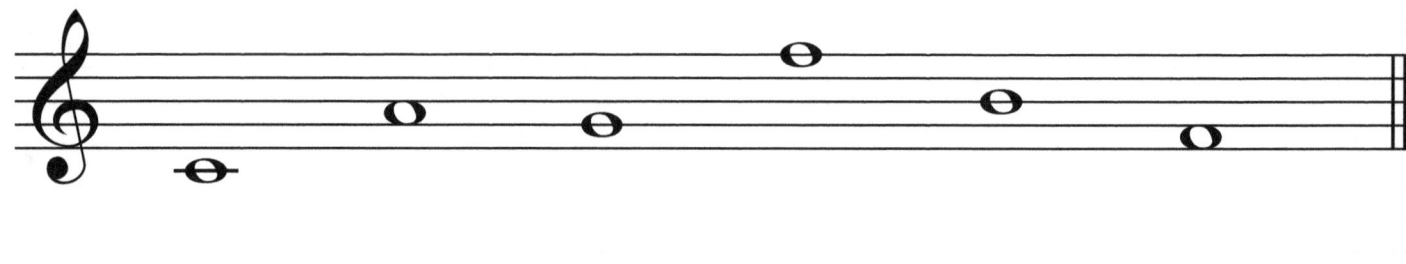

___   ___   ___   ___   ___   ___

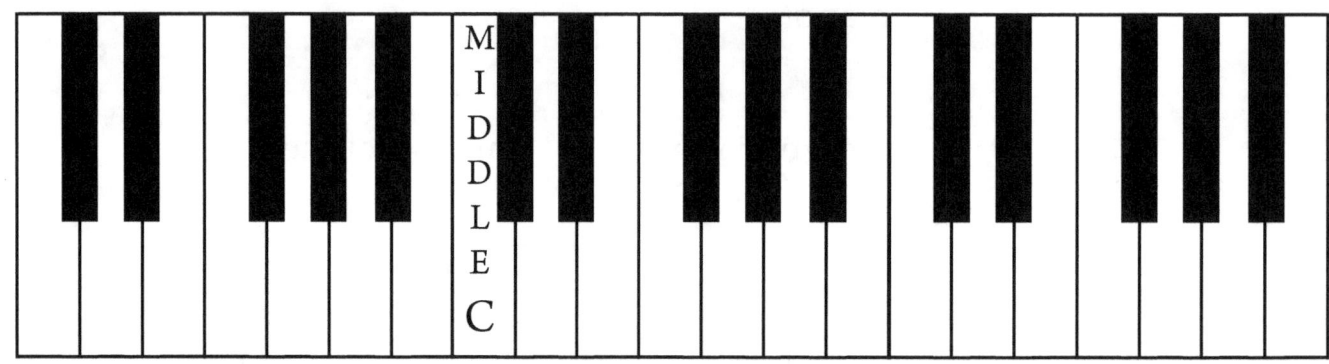

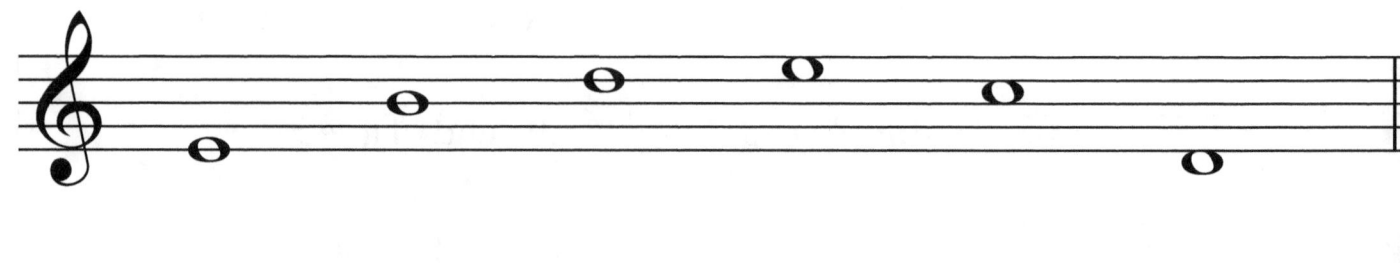

___   ___   ___   ___   ___   ___

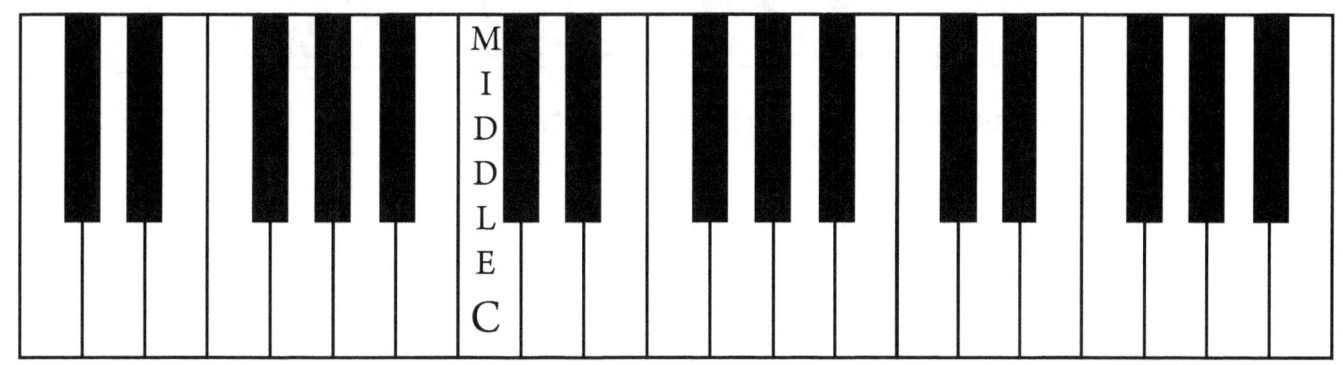

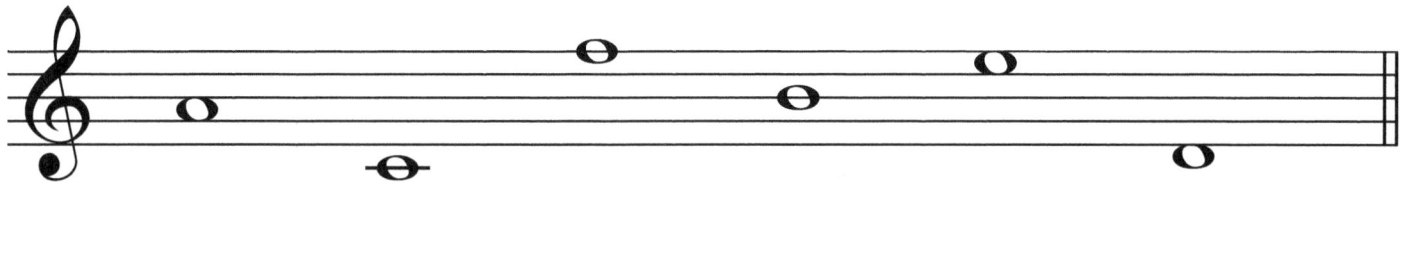

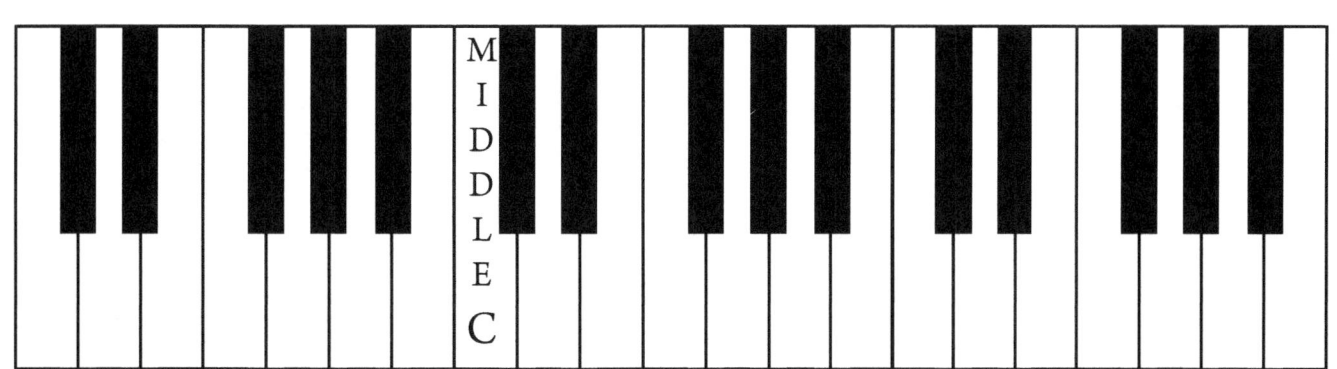

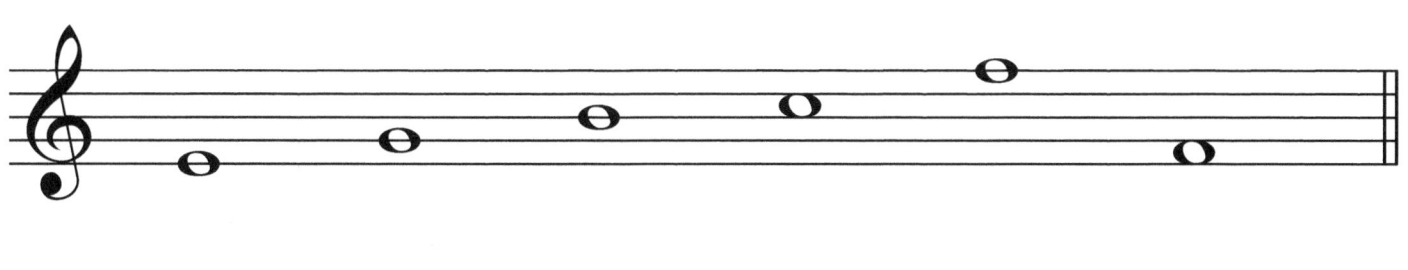

SPELLING FUN

1. Spell these words using notes on the treble staff.

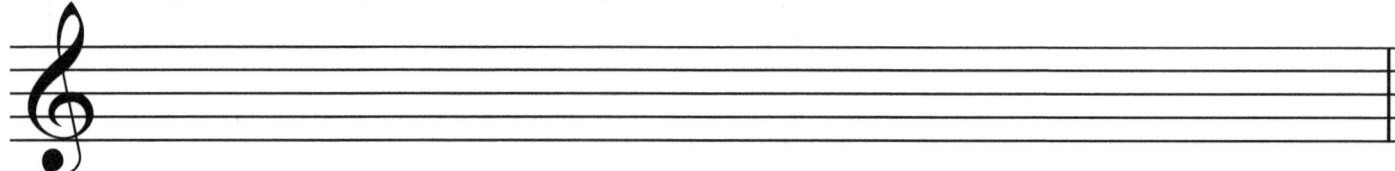

EGG   CAGE   BEG   ADD

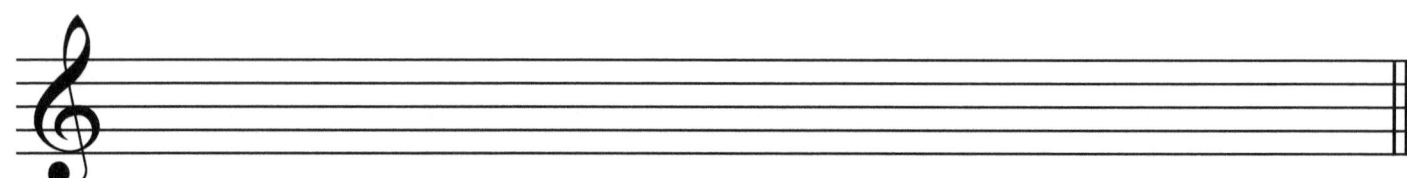

BAGGAGE   CAB   DAD

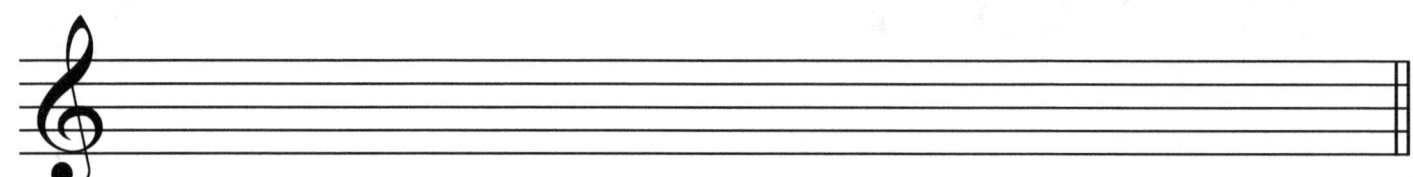

FEED   DAB   GAG   BAD

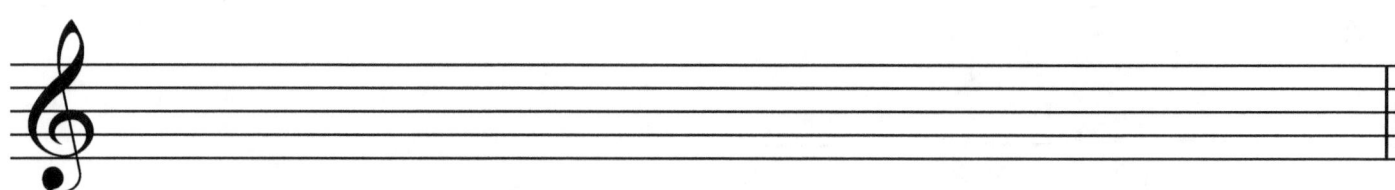

FACE   EDGE   BADGE

2. Name these notes. They spell words.

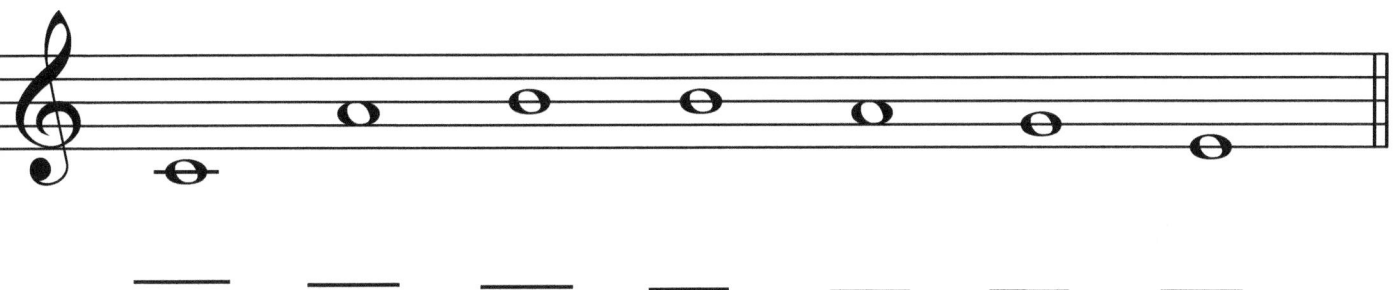

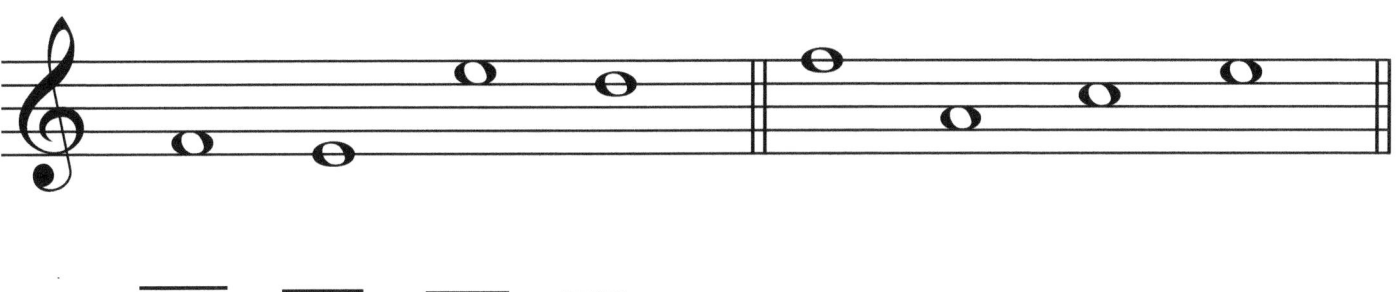

MATCHING FUN

1. Draw lines matching the signs with their names.

mf   piano

           mezzo piano

p   forte

f   mezzo forte

mp   ritardando

rit.   double bar

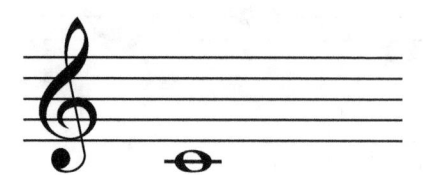

           middle C

2. Draw lines matching the notes with the letters.

Wolfgang Amadeus Mozart (1756-1791)

Mozart was born in Salzburg, Austria. He began performing and composing music at an early age. He wrote a minuet at age six. His Violin Sonata, Op. 1, no. 1, his first published, work appeared in Paris in 1764, when he was only eight.

Mozart spent his youth travelling across Europe with his father and his older sister, Nannerl. The wealthy nobility were amazed at his musical skill, and he won their hearts with his youthful charm. By the time he was eleven, Mozart had written symphonies, chamber music, songs, and a short opera Bastien et Bastienne.

Mozart eventually settled in Vienna and continued to compose and perform. His music is filled with wonderful melodies and a great variety of moods and feelings. Today he is particularly admired for his operas, symphonies, and piano music.

Notes on the Bass Staff

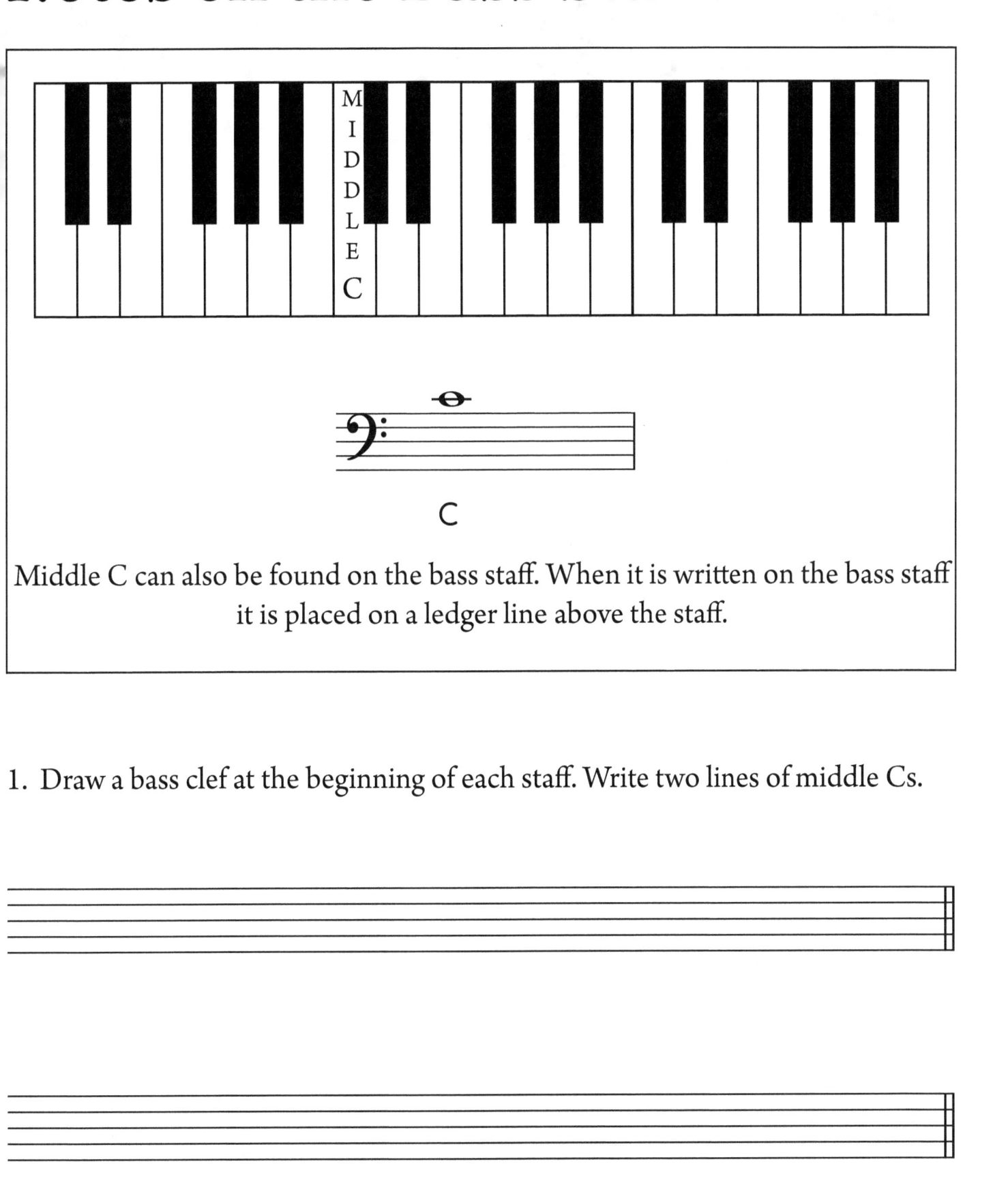

C

Middle C can also be found on the bass staff. When it is written on the bass staff it is placed on a ledger line above the staff.

1. Draw a bass clef at the beginning of each staff. Write two lines of middle Cs.

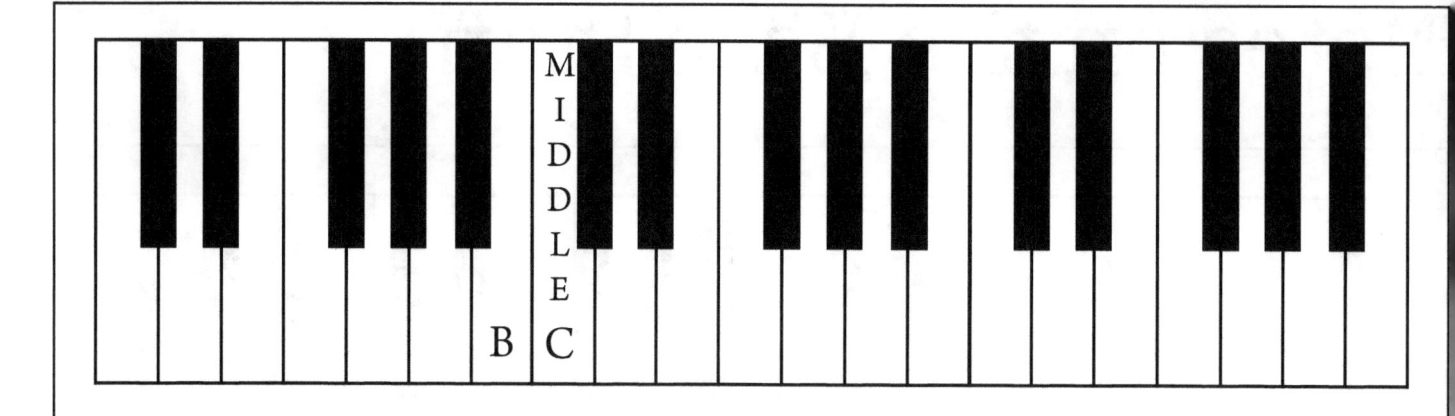

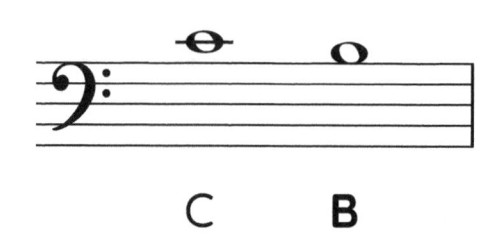

The note found just below middle C in the bass clef is B.
It sits on top of the five lines of the bass staff.

1. Draw a bass clef and write a line of Bs.

2. Name these notes.

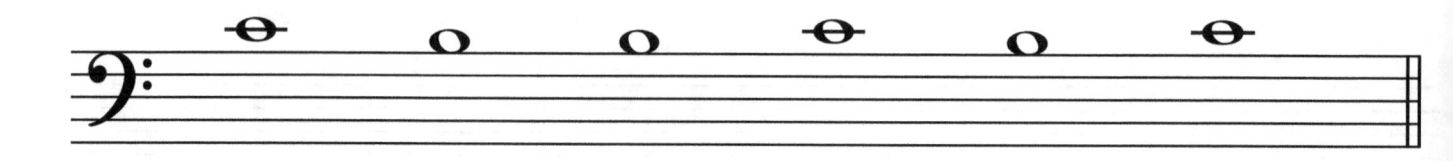

Here are the notes on the five lines of the bass staff:

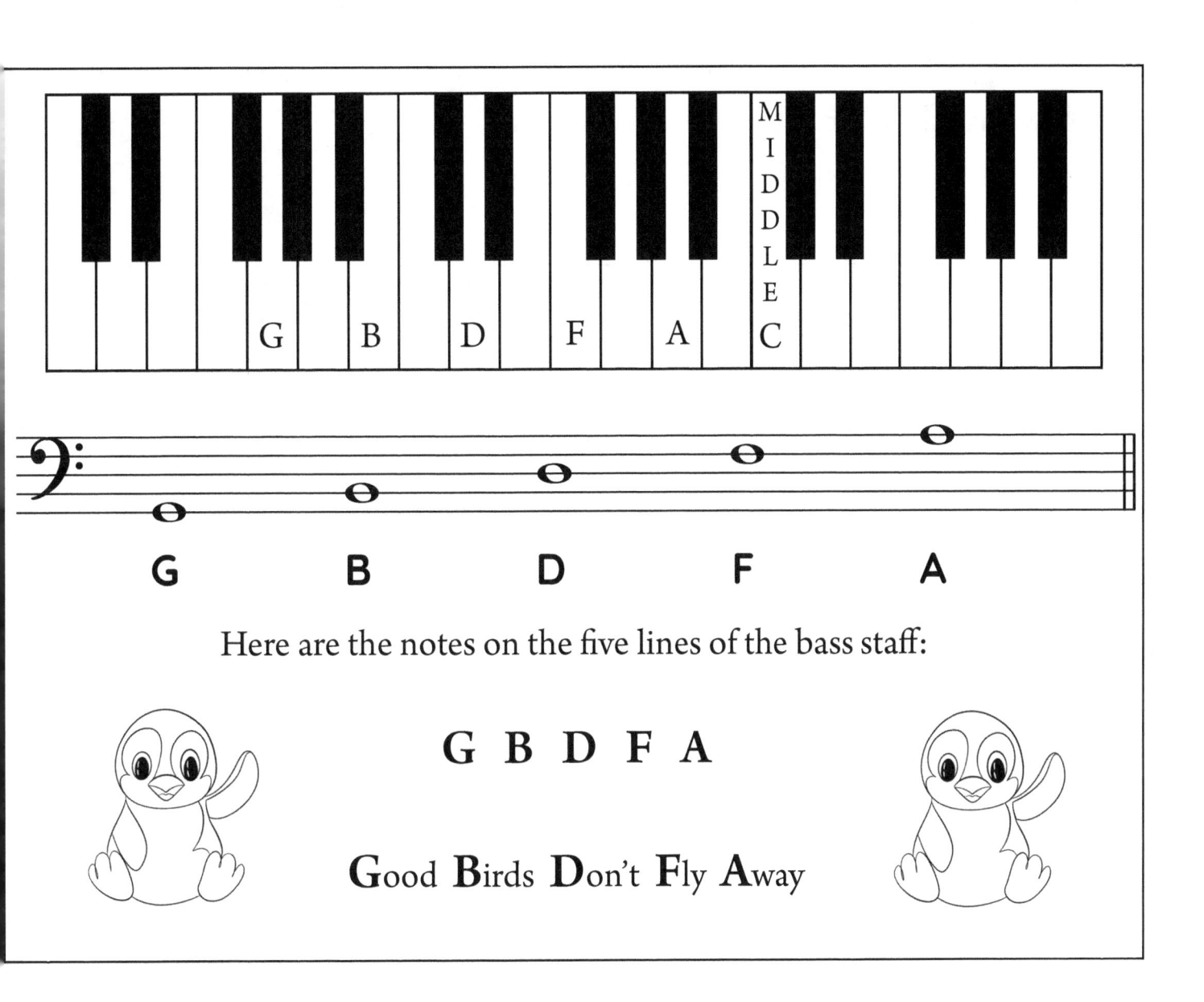

G B D F A

Good **B**irds **D**on't **F**ly **A**way

1. Name these notes. When you are finished, play them!

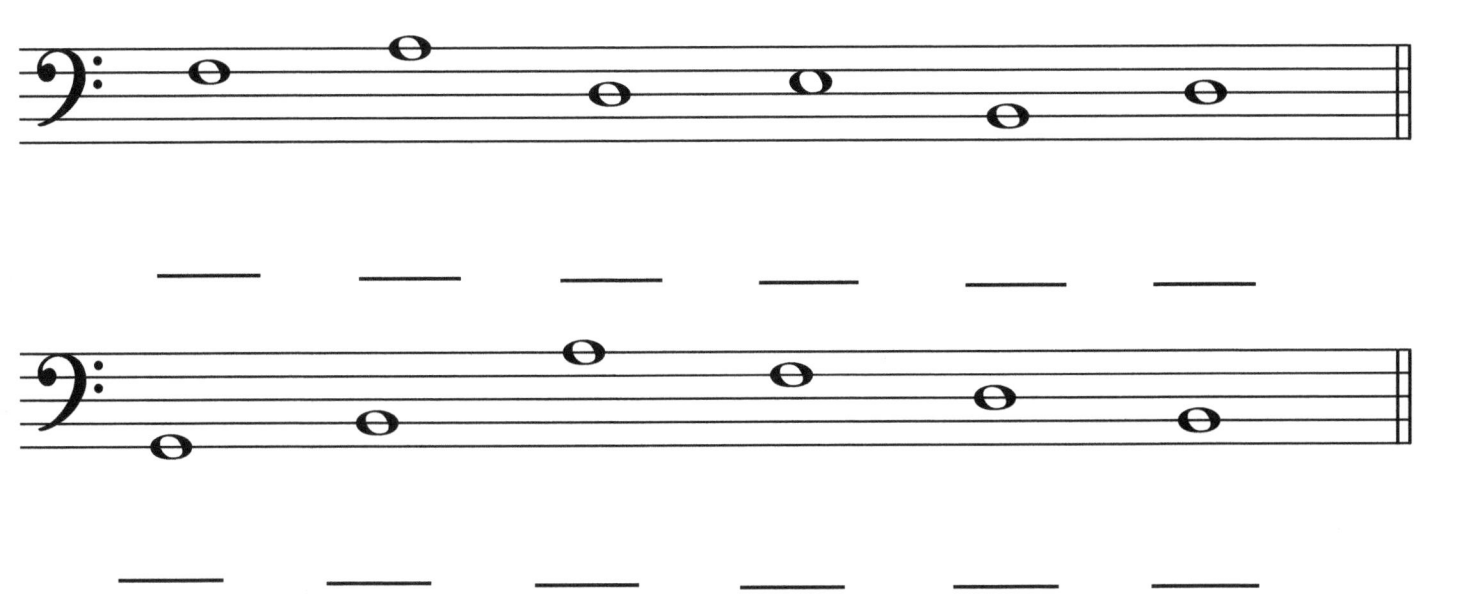

2. Draw bass clefs. Write these notes on lines.

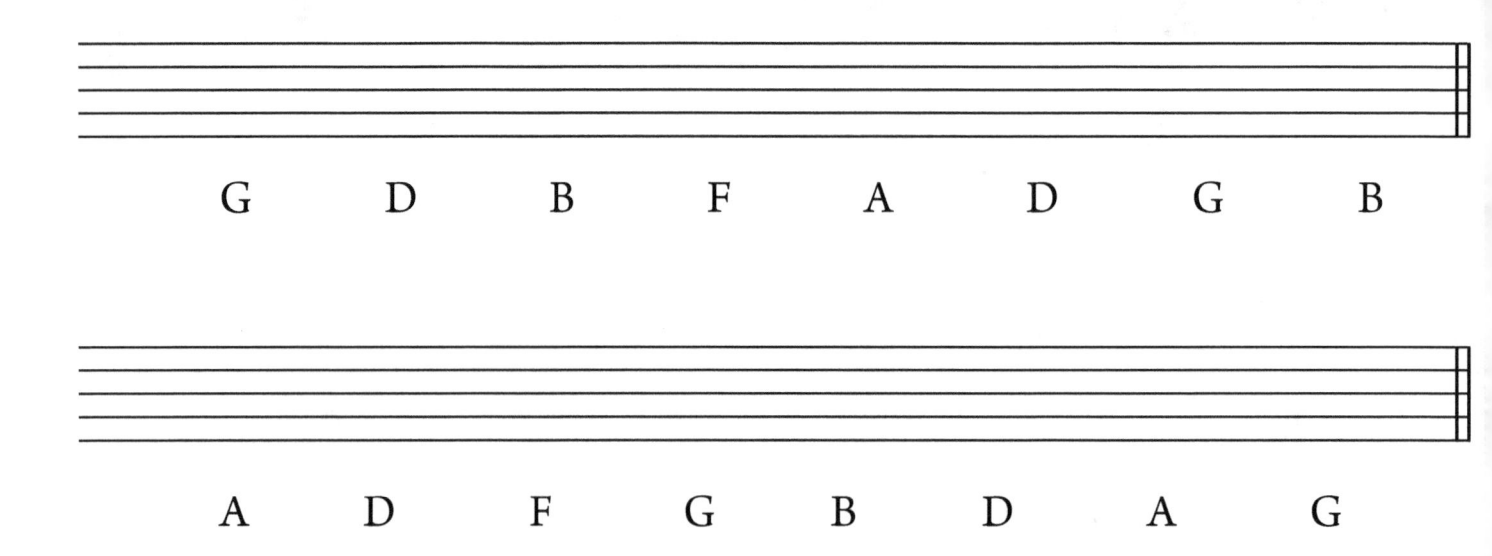

G   D   B   F   A   D   G   B

A   D   F   G   B   D   A   G

3. Name these notes.

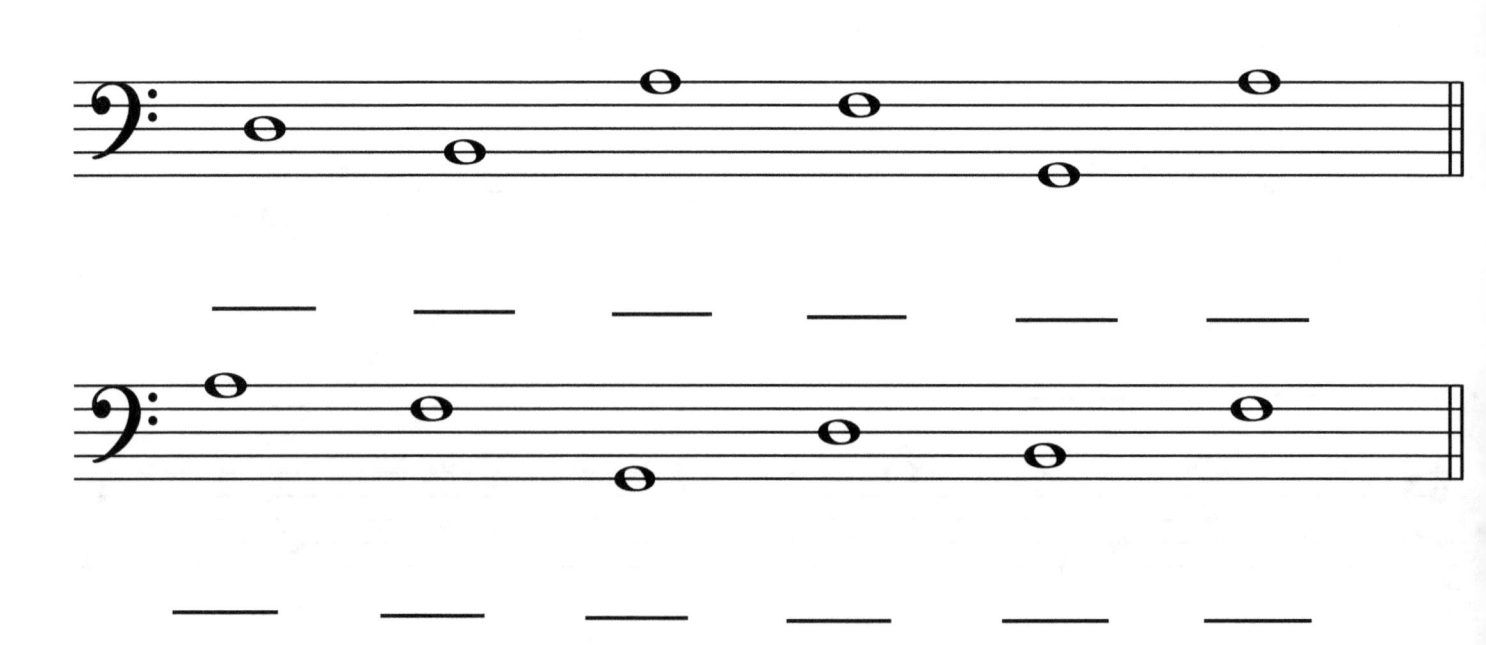

A C E G

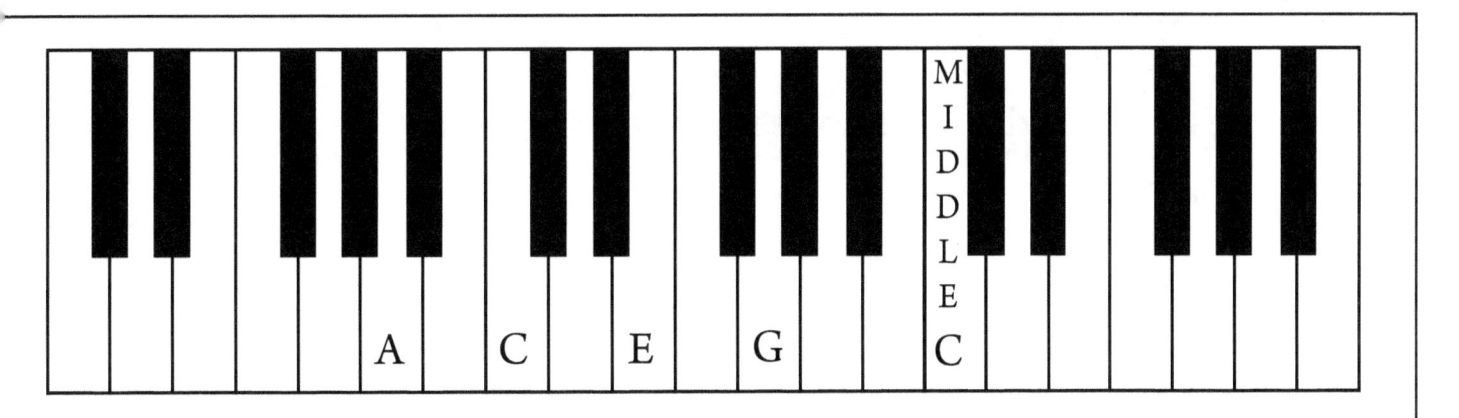

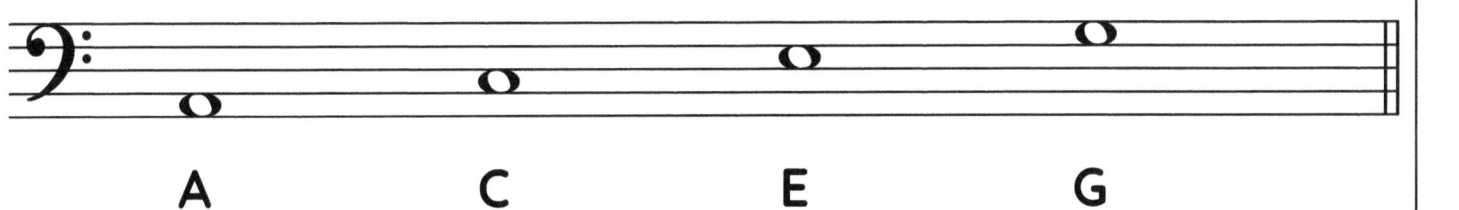

Here are the notes on the four spaces of the bass staff:

A C E G

Alligators **C**an't **E**at **G**umballs

1. Name these notes. When you are finished, play them!

40

2. Draw bass clefs. Write these notes in spaces.

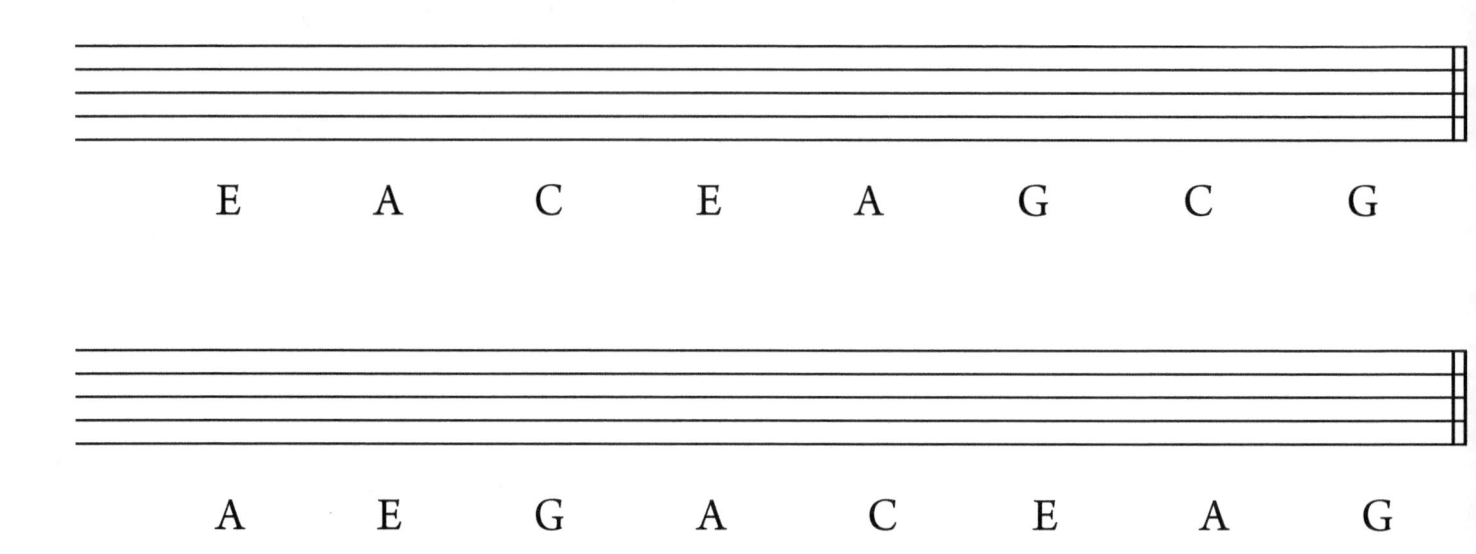

```
        E     A     C     E     A     G     C     G


        A     E     G     A     C     E     A     G
```

3. Name these notes.

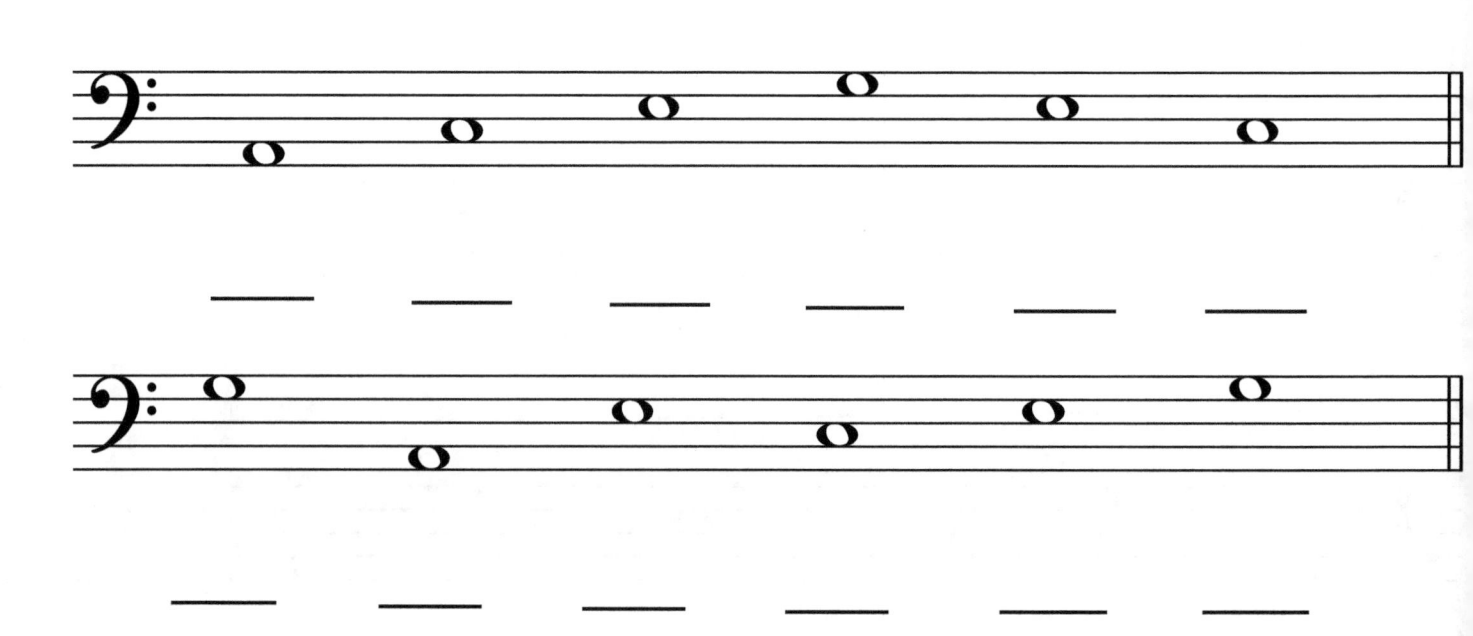

4. Write these notes in the bass staff. Use both lines and spaces.
   When you have finished, play them.

Don't forget to draw bass clefs!

G   A   B   D   E   F   middleC   G

B   A   G   F   B   E   G   D

middle C   G   A   B   D   E   F   C

G   F   E   B   A   B   C   D

5. Name these notes.

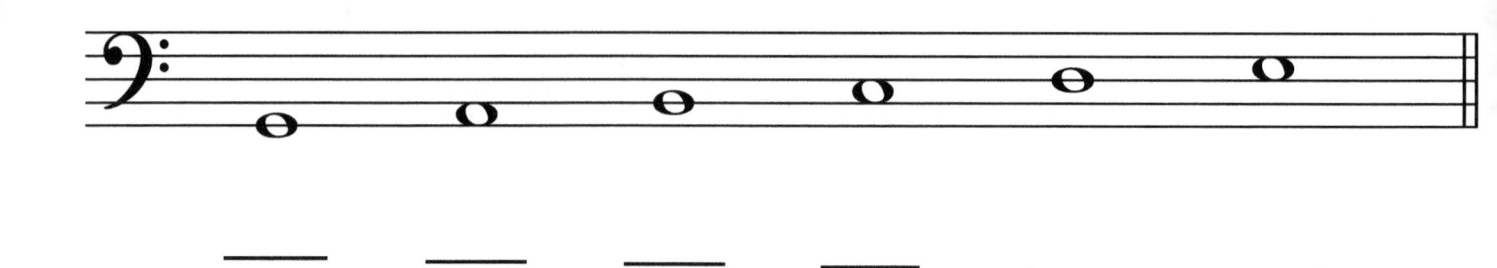

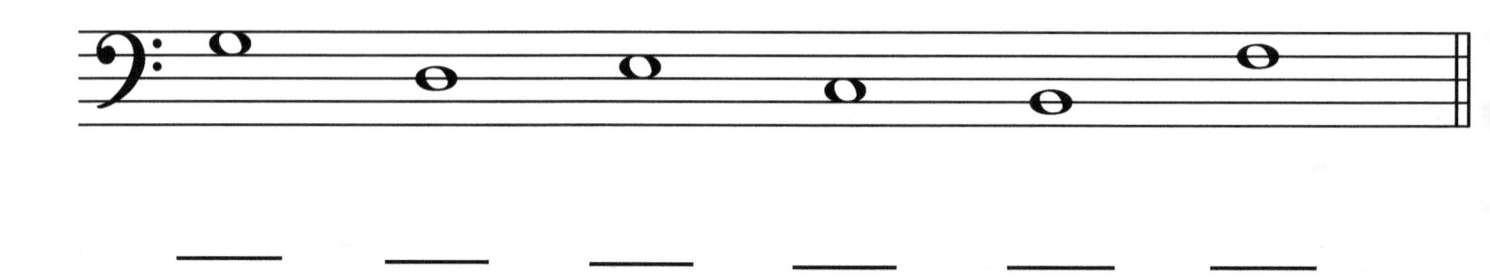

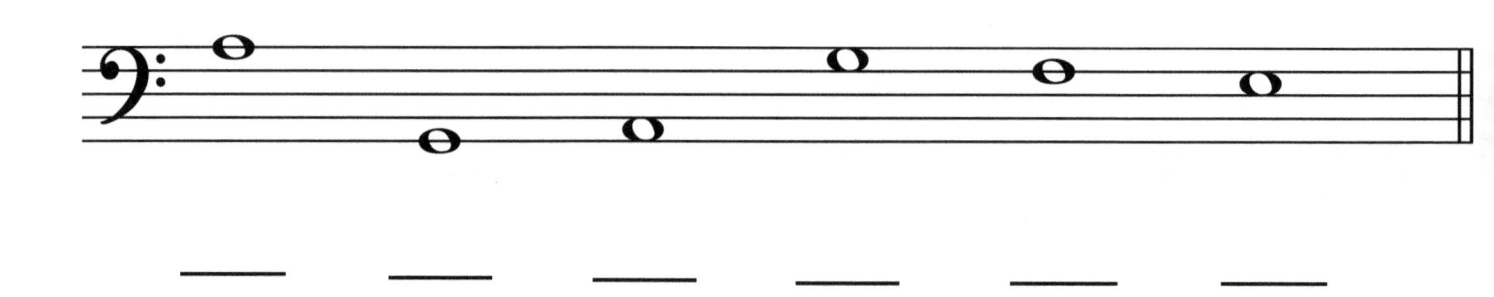

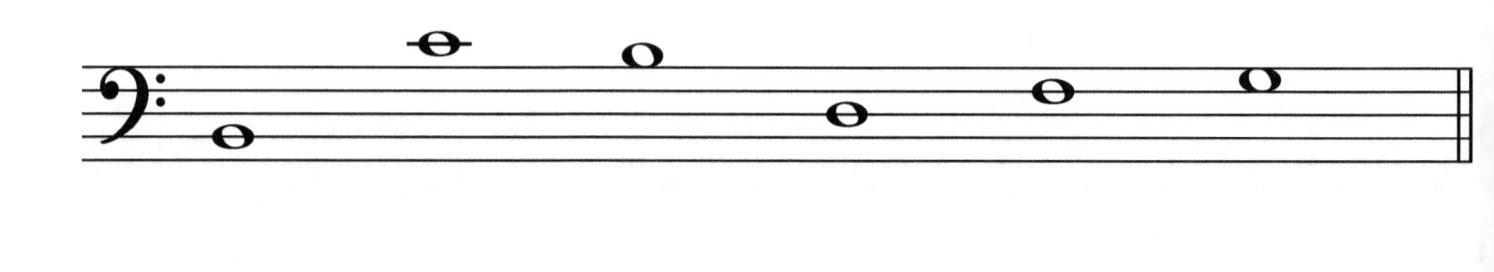

6. Beginning with low G (line 1), write all the bass clef notes ascending.
   Write the letter name under each note.

7. Beginning with middle C, write all the bass clef notes descending.
   Write the letter name under each note.

Musical Signs

(crescendo symbol)	crescendo	becoming louder
(diminuendo symbol)	diminuendo	becoming softer
(fermata symbol)	fermata	pause
(staccato symbol)	staccato	play notes short and detached
(tie symbol)	tie	hold for the value of both notes
(repeat sign symbol)	repeat sign	repeat the notes between the signs

8. Name these notes. Draw lines connecting them to the keys on the keyboards.

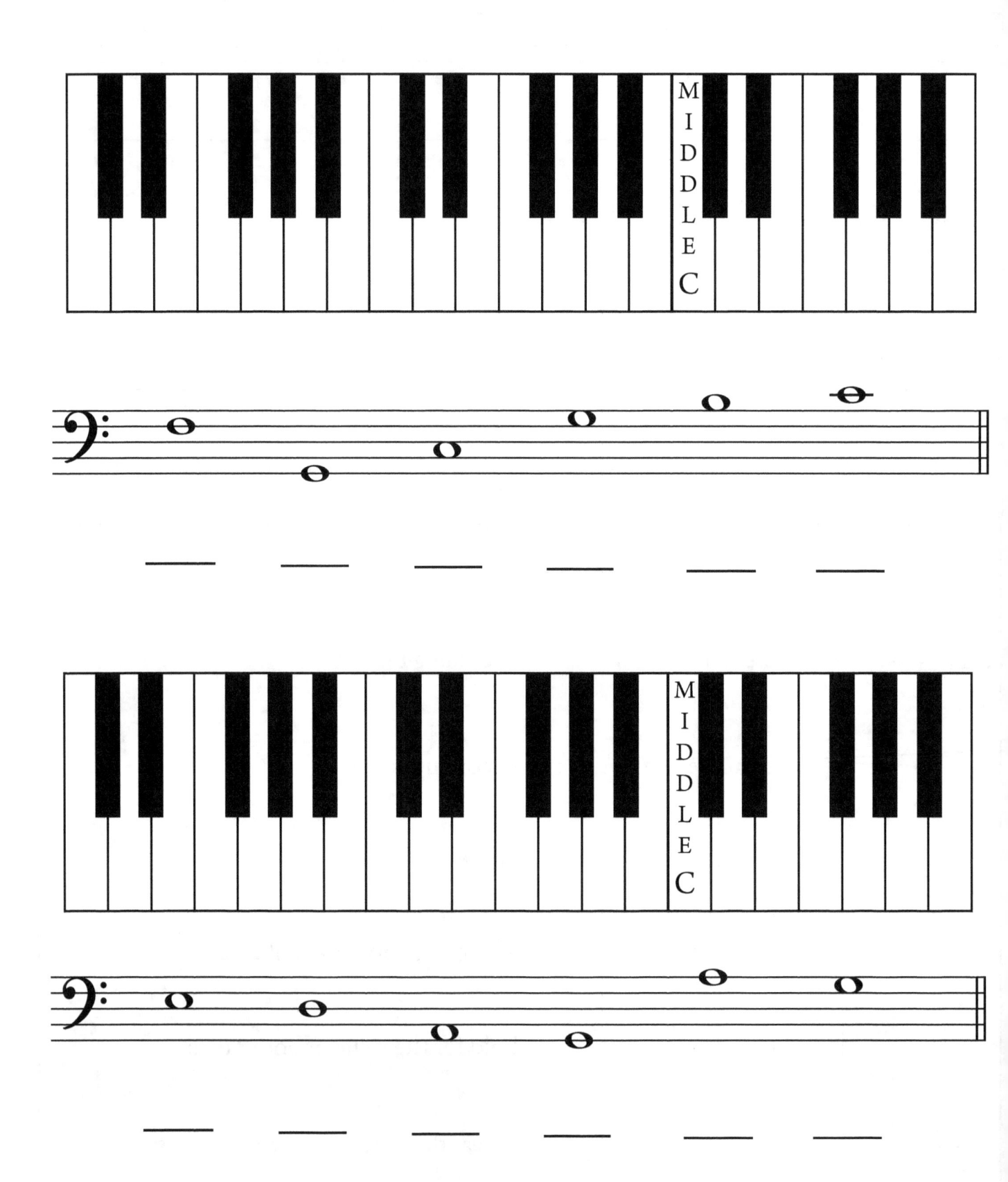

46

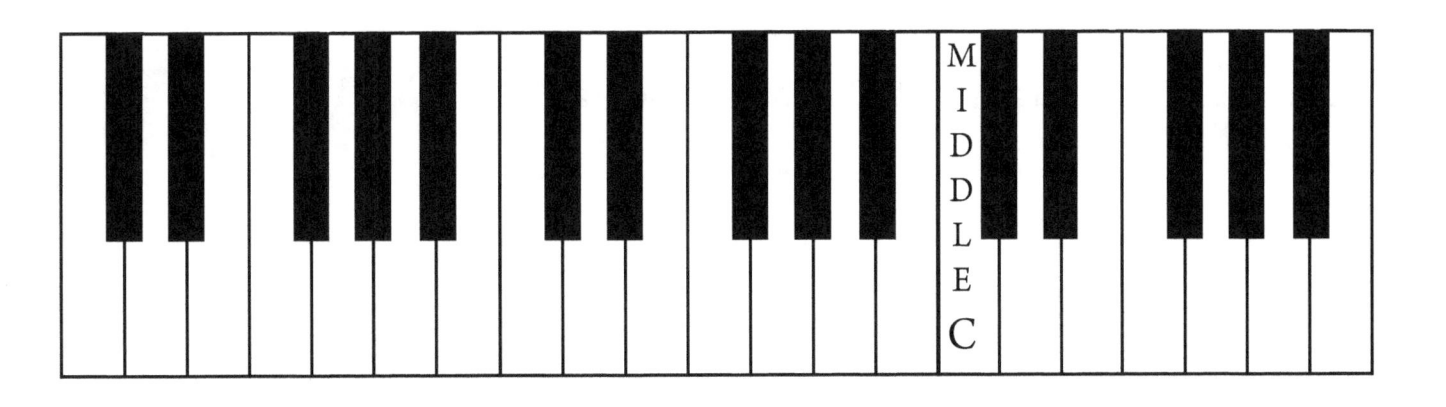

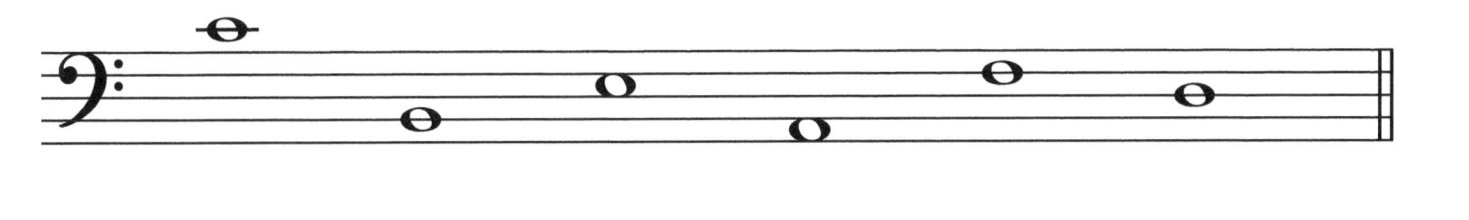

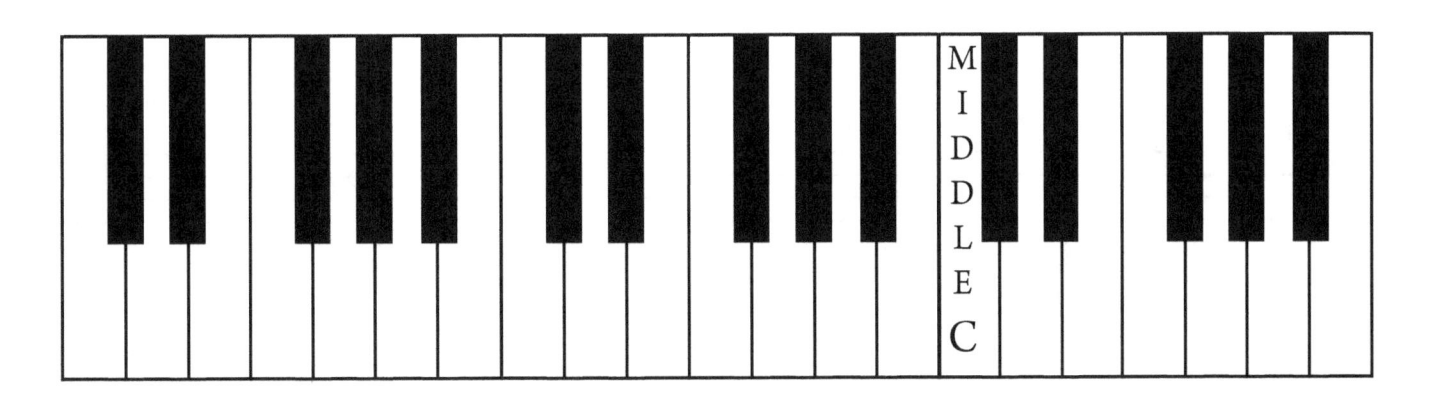

SPELLING FUN

1. Spell these words using notes on the treble staff.

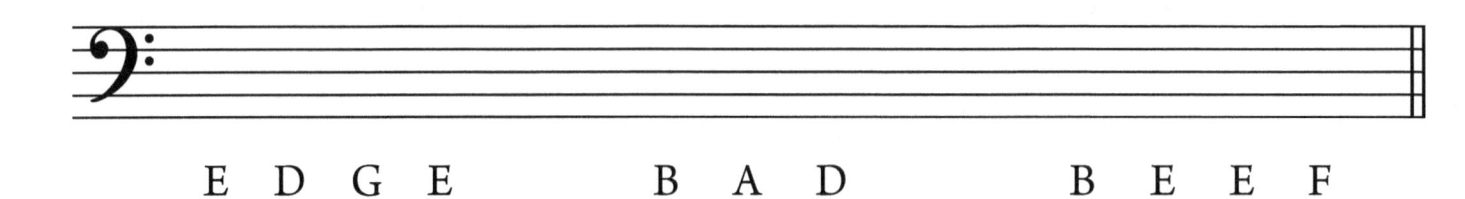

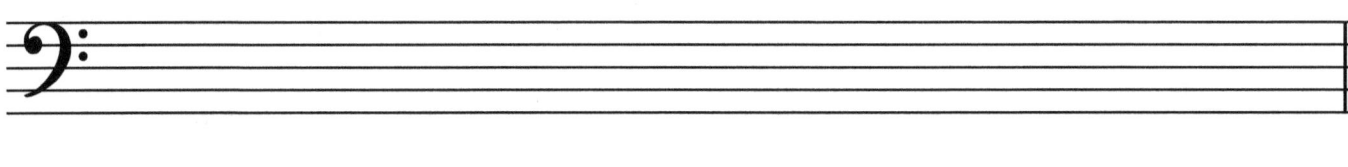

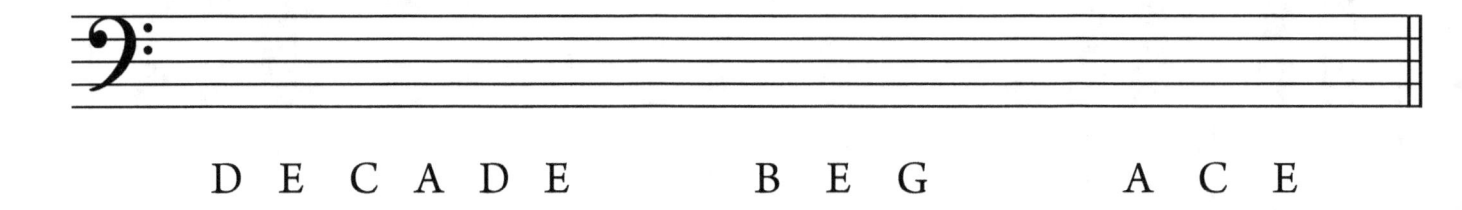

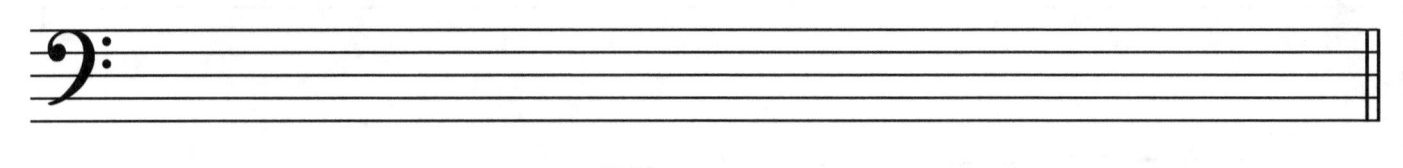

𝄢

    E D G E   B A D   B E E F

𝄢

    D A B   F A C E   B A D G E

𝄢

    D E C A D E   B E G   A C E

𝄢

    E G G   B E E   F A D E

2. Name these notes. They spell words.

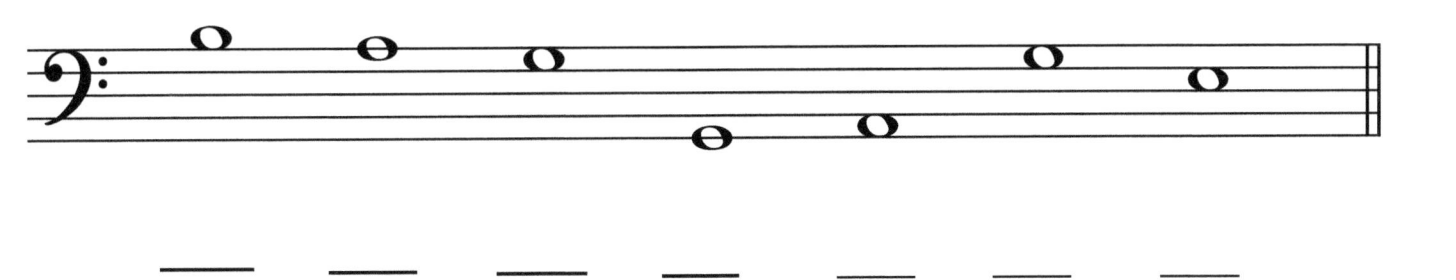

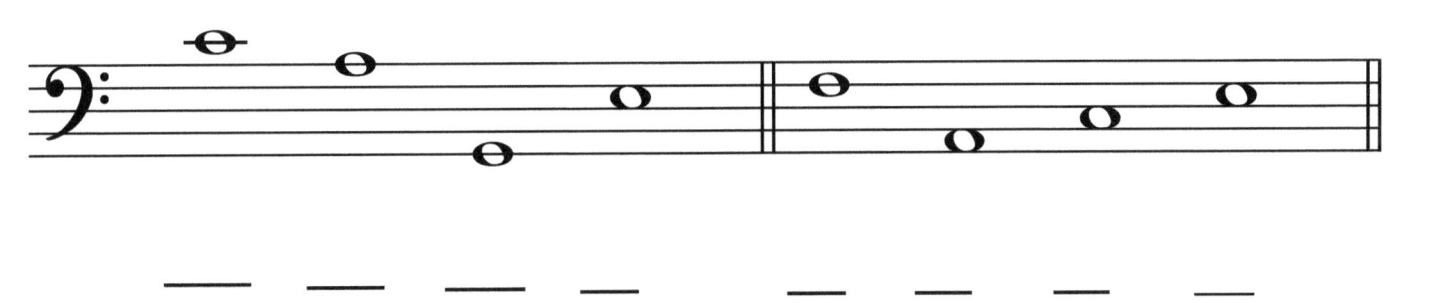

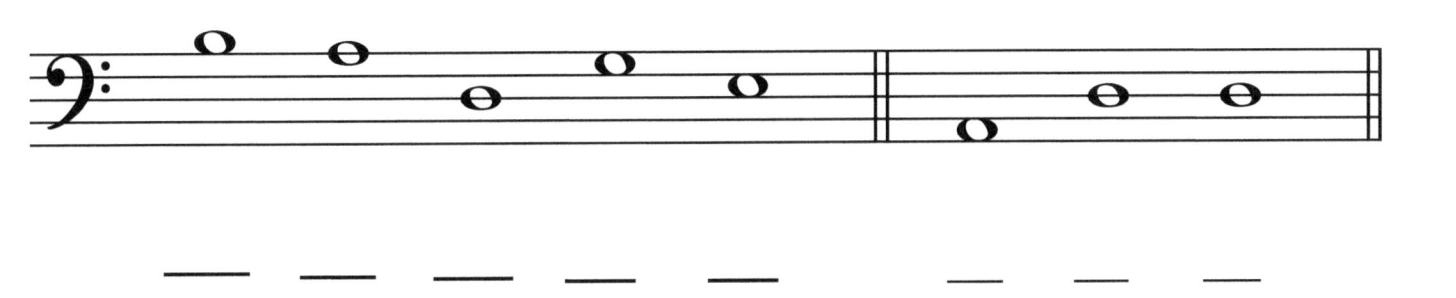

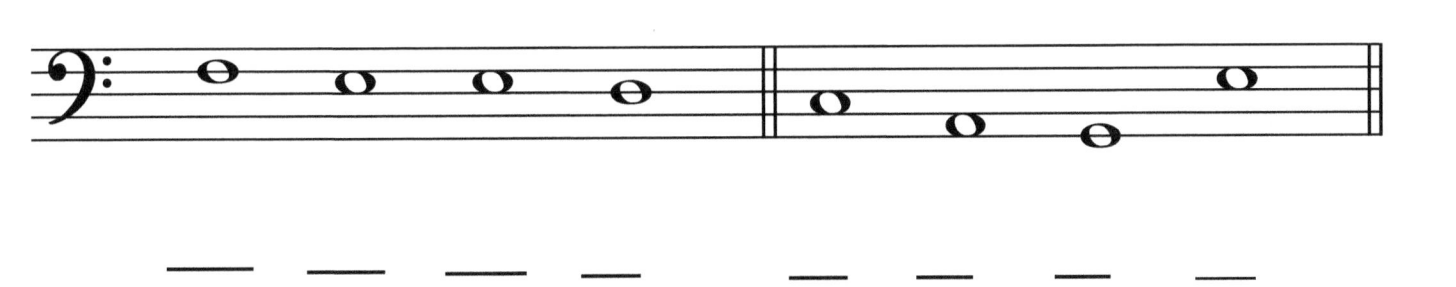

MATCHING FUN

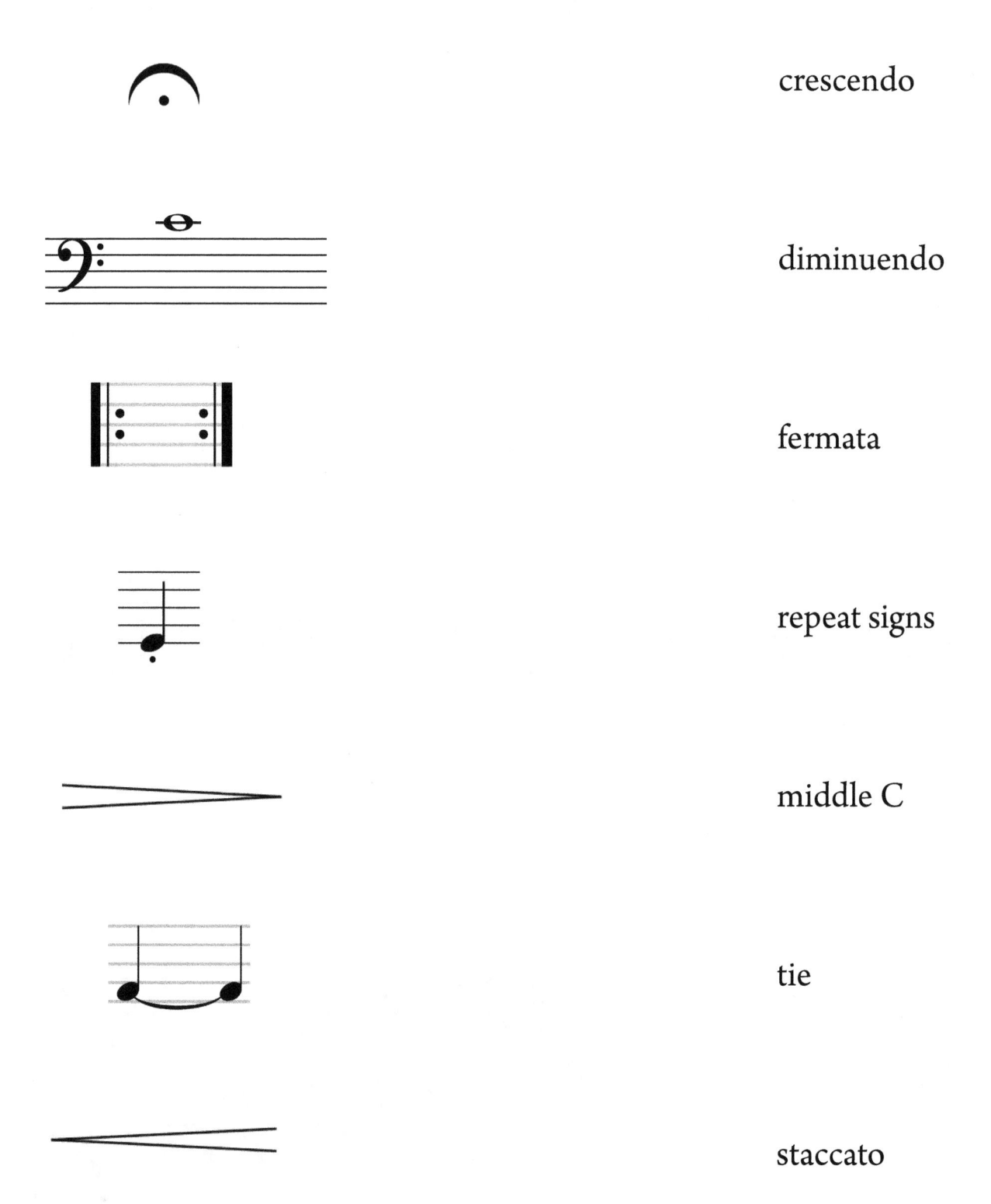

1. Draw lines matching the signs with their names.

crescendo

diminuendo

fermata

repeat signs

middle C

tie

staccato

2. Draw lines matching the notes with the letters.

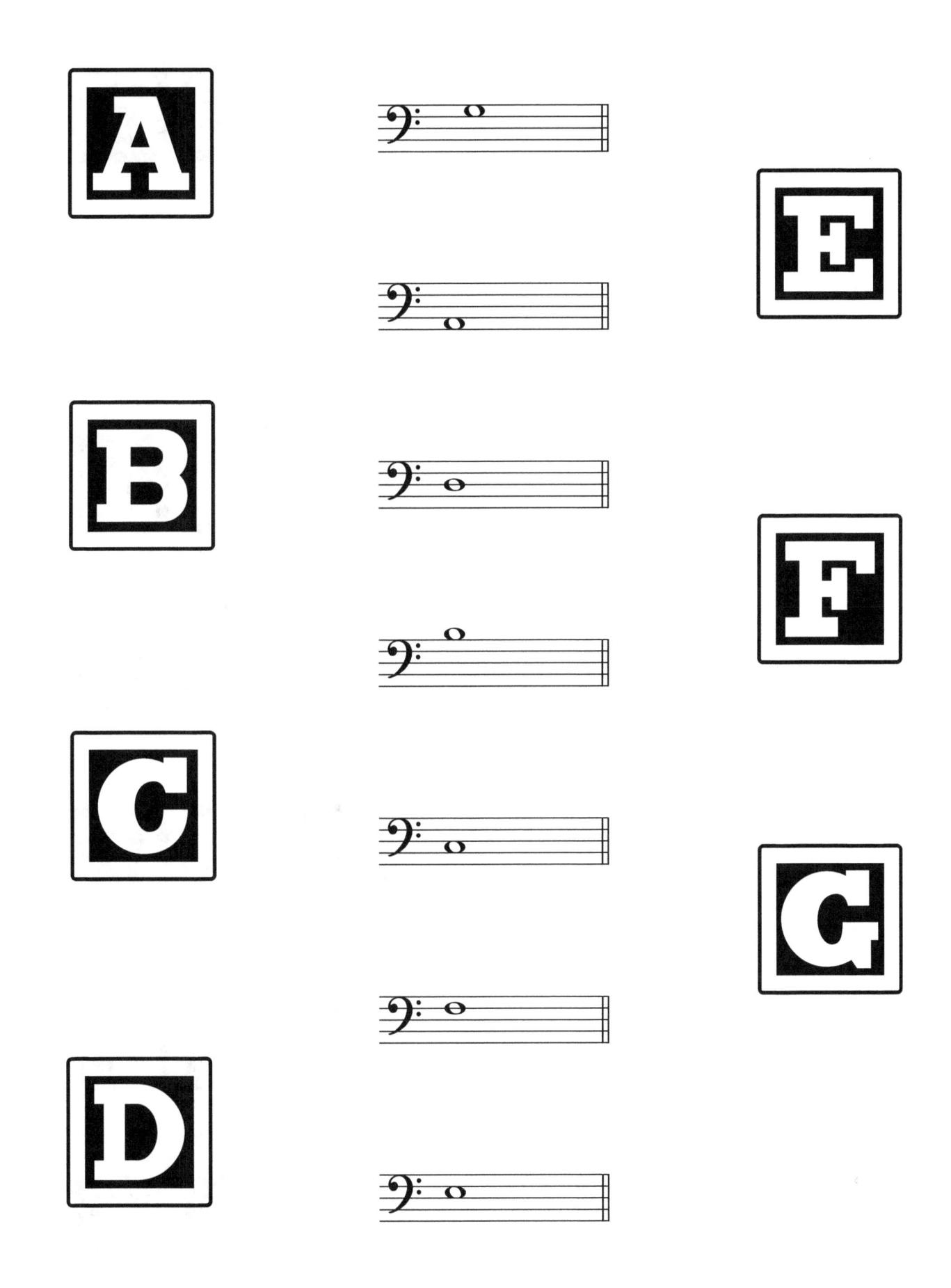

3. Draw lines matching the groups of notes with the letters.

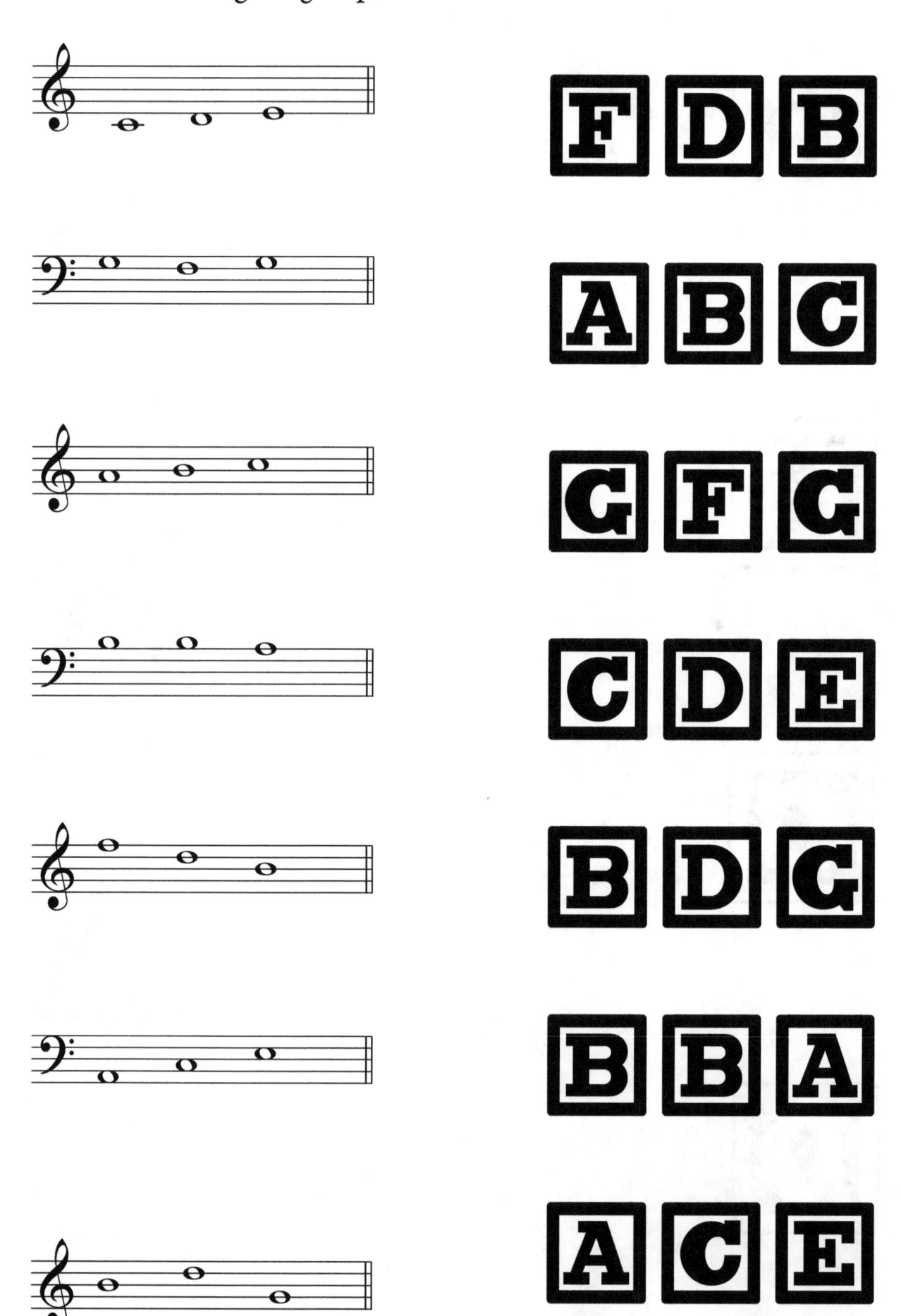

Ludwig van Beethoven (1770-1827)

Beethoven was born in Bonn, which is in Germany. His grandfather and his father were court musicians. As a child, Beethoven studied piano, organ, violin, and viola. He also began to write music and became an avid composer.

In 1792, he moved to Vienna where he took composition lessons with Haydn. Beethoven quickly became a popular pianist and composer... in spite of his gruff character.

Less than ten years later, Beethoven began to lose his hearing. But even in his deafness he explored new sounds in his music. He wrote down his musical ideas in sketchbooks. These books are a diary of his musical life. Beethoven is probably one of the greatest composers of all time.

The Grand Staff

The treble and bass combine to make the grand staff.
The staves are joined by a straight line and a curved brace.

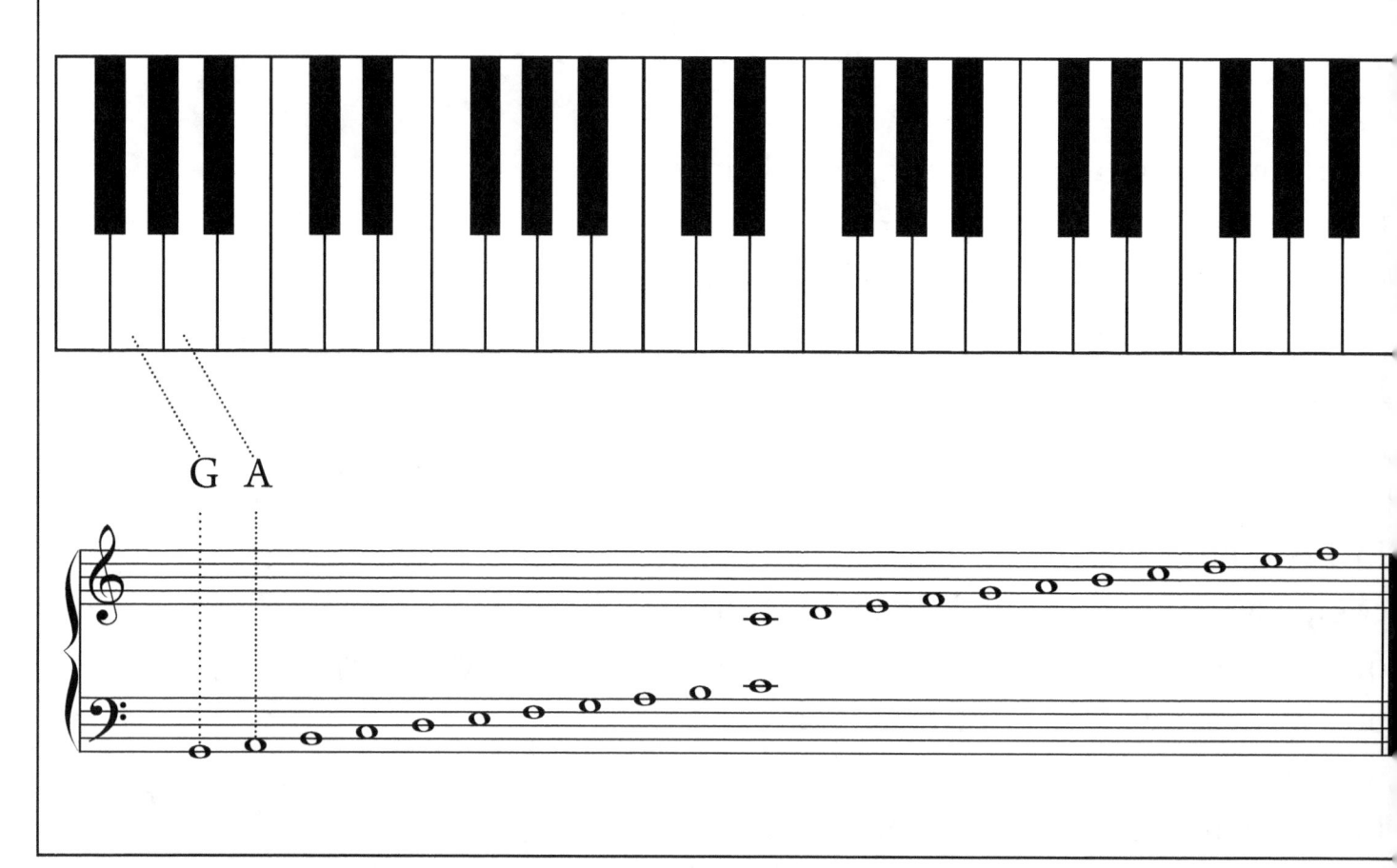

1. Print the name of each note above the staff and draw lines connecting the letter names to the keys.

2. Practice drawing grand staves drawing the line, brace, and the treble and bass clefs.

3. Draw a grand staff. Write all the notes on the grand staff. Begin with the highest line in the treble clef. Write the letter name under each note.

4. Draw a grand staff. Write all the notes on it. Begin with the lowest line in the bass clef. Draw lines from the notes to the keys on the keyboard. Write the letter names on the keys.

5. Write the following notes on the grand staff.

| three different Gs | three different As | three different Fs | three different Ds |

| three different Bs | three different Cs | three different Es | C on a line |

| G in a space | G on a line | A in a space | D on a line |

6. Name these notes.

Franz Liszt
(1811-1886)

Liszt was born in Raiding, Hungary in 1811. His father began teaching him music when he was six years old. Liszt gave his first public piano recital when he was nine. He knew Beethoven and Schubert and was a close friend to Chopin

Liszt was a great piano virtuoso and wrote many virtuosic pieces for piano. He composed over 400 original works. He also wrote 900 transcriptions which are arrangements of other compositions or songs.

Notes and Time

Different kinds of notes show different lengths or durations of sound. Here are six different kinds of notes.

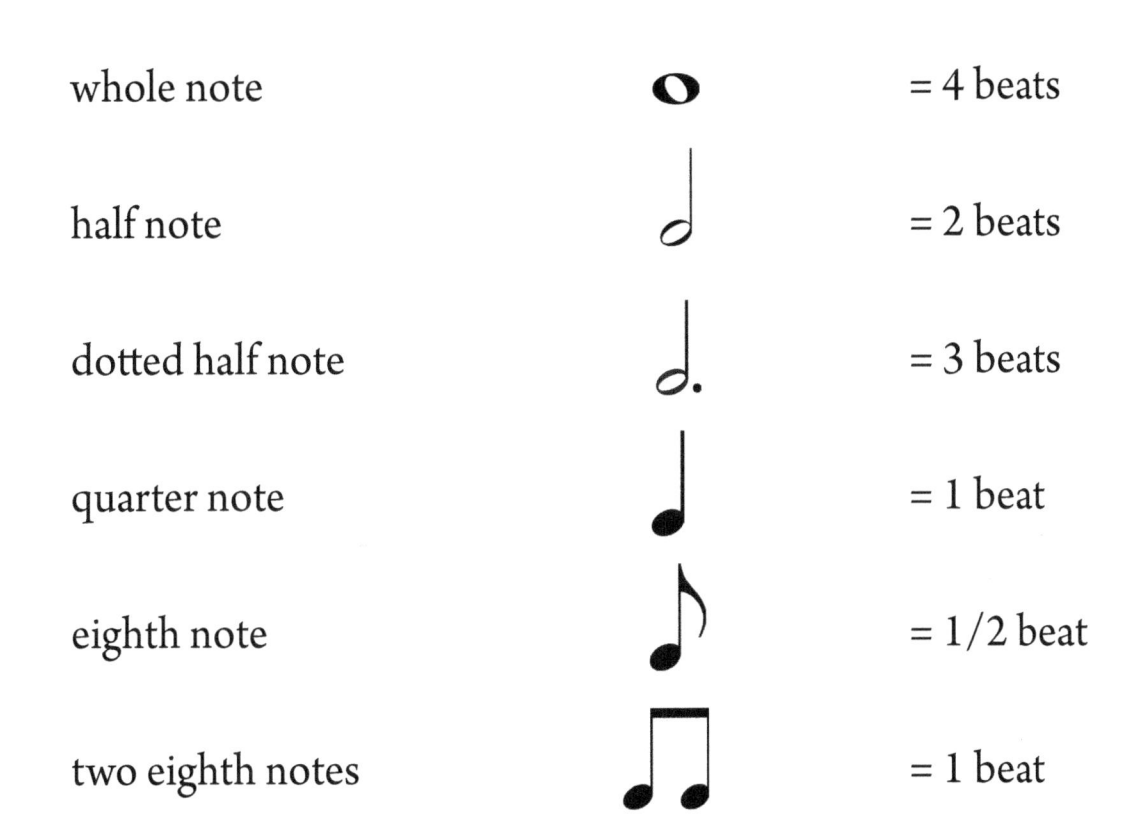

whole note	𝅝	= 4 beats
half note	𝅗𝅥	= 2 beats
dotted half note	𝅗𝅥.	= 3 beats
quarter note	♩	= 1 beat
eighth note	♪	= 1/2 beat
two eighth notes	♫	= 1 beat

The names of these notes indicate their values.

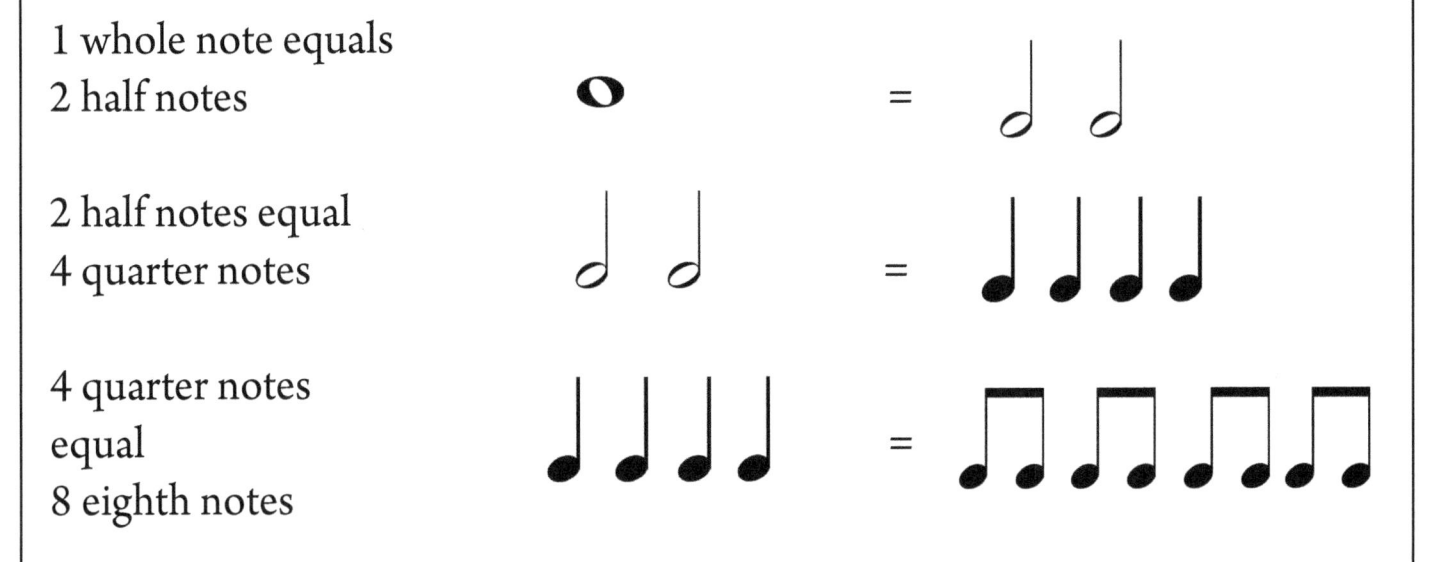

1 whole note equals
2 half notes   𝅝 = 𝅗𝅥 𝅗𝅥

2 half notes equal
4 quarter notes   𝅗𝅥 𝅗𝅥 = ♩ ♩ ♩ ♩

4 quarter notes equal
8 eighth notes   ♩ ♩ ♩ ♩ = ♫ ♫ ♫ ♫

1. Write whole notes.

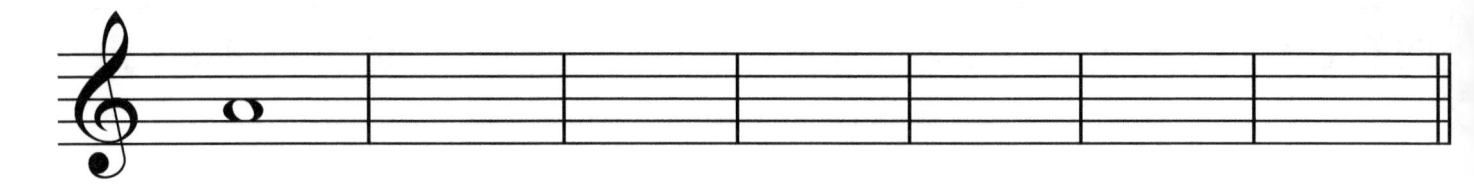

2. Write dotted half notes.

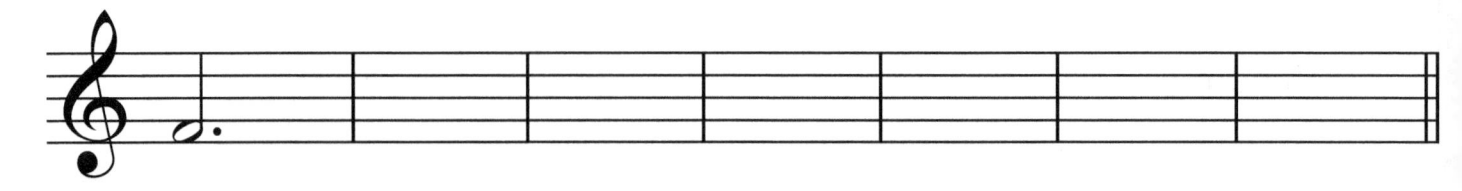

3. Write half notes.

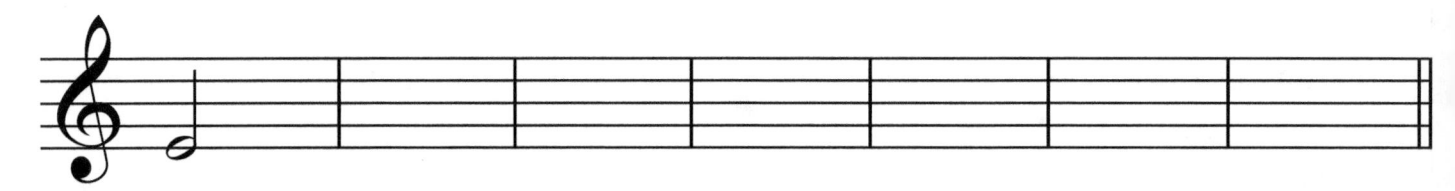

4. Write quarter notes.

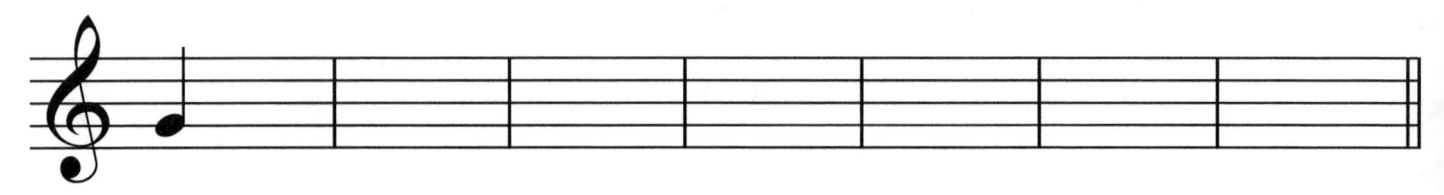

5. Write eighth notes.

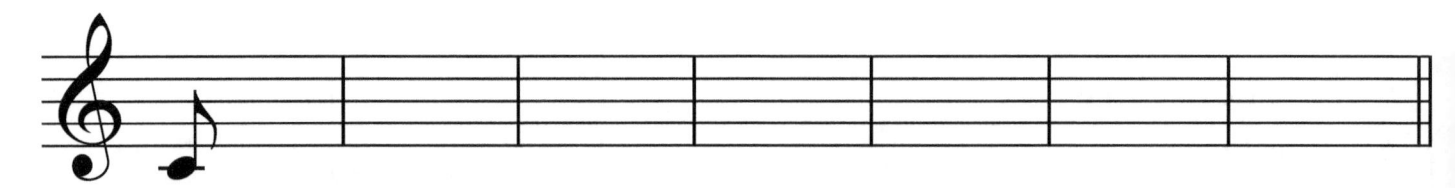

6. Write pairs of eighth notes.

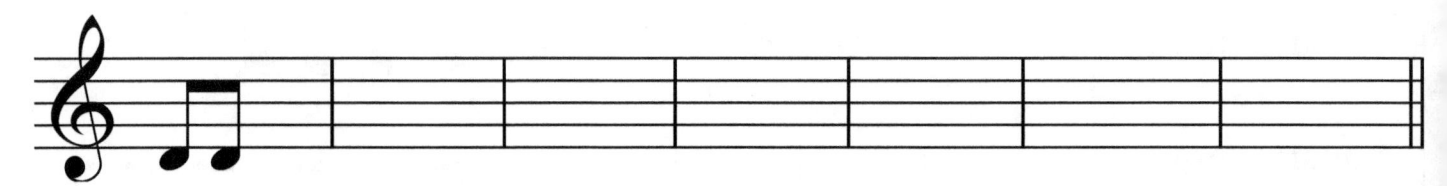

7. Write the following notes in the boxes below.

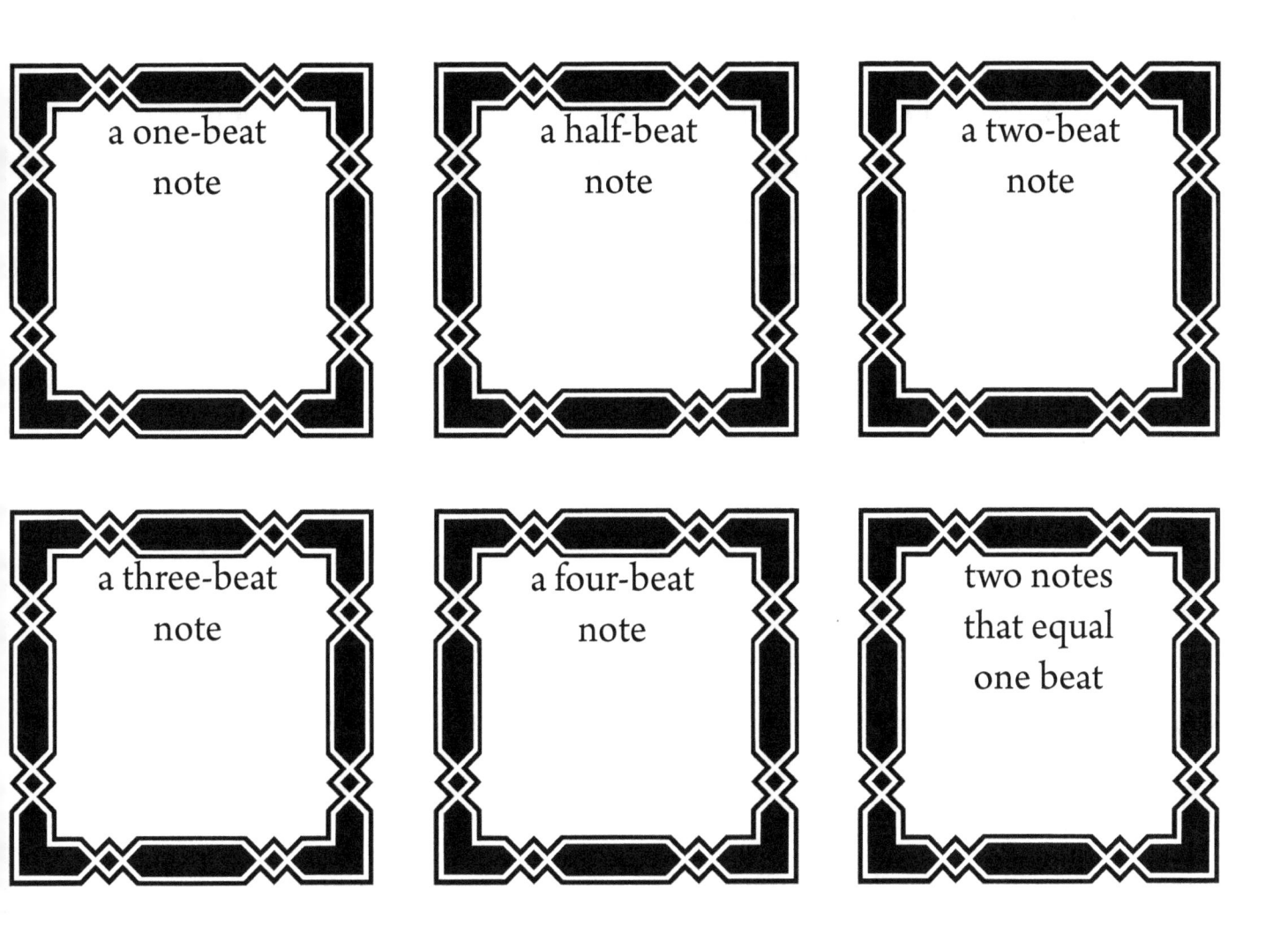

| a one-beat note | a half-beat note | a two-beat note |

| a three-beat note | a four-beat note | two notes that equal one beat |

8. Write the number of beats that each note or pair of notes receives.

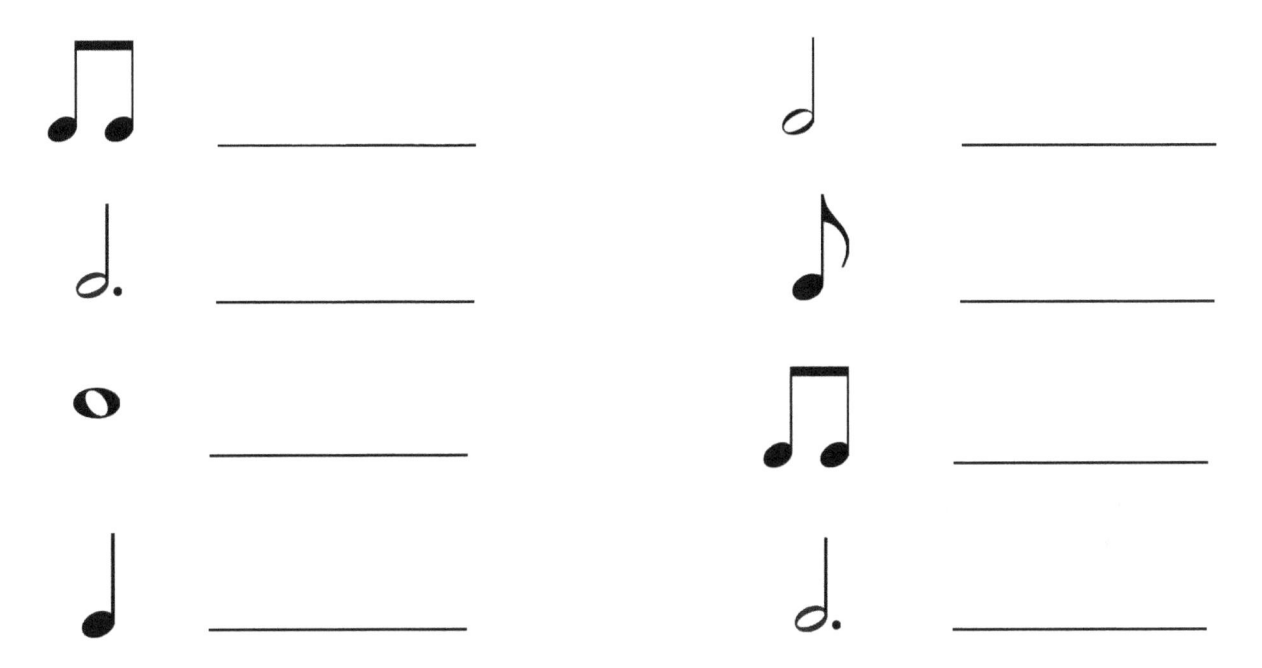

♫ _____   𝅗𝅥 _____

𝅗𝅥. _____   ♪ _____

𝅝 _____   ♫ _____

♩ _____   𝅗𝅥. _____

Rests

Different kinds of rests show different lengths or durations of silence. Here are four different kinds of rests.

whole rest = 4 beats

half rest = 2 beats

quarter rest = 1 beat

eighth rest = 1/2 beat

A rest has the same value as a note with the same name.

1 whole note equals
1 whole rest

1 half note equals
1 half rest

1 quarter note equals
1 quarter rest

1 eighth note equals
1 eighth rest

1. Write whole rests.

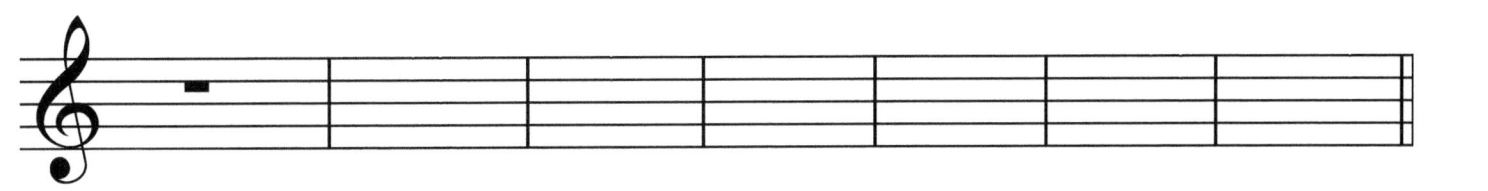

2. Write half rests.

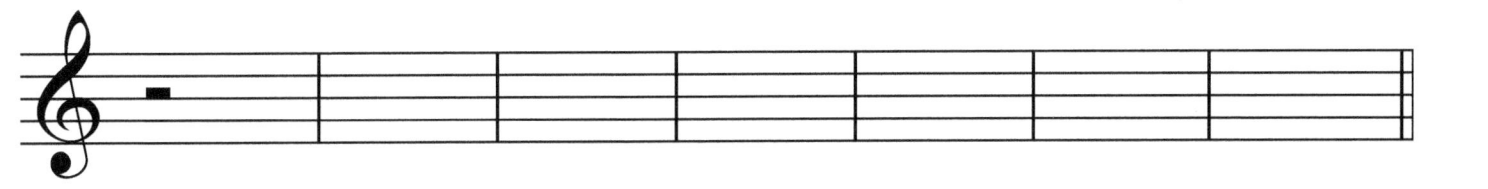

3. Write quarter rests.

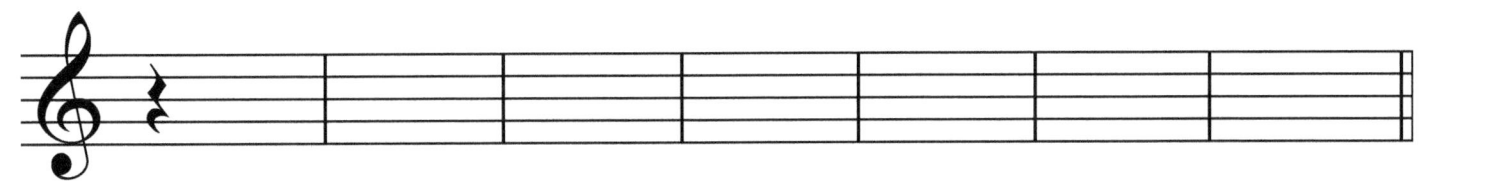

4. Write eighth rests.

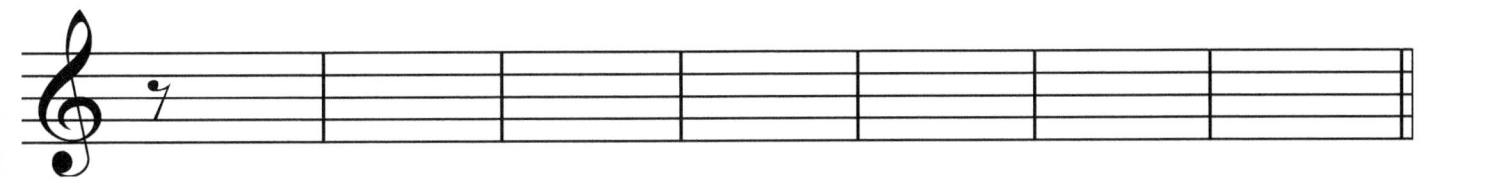

5. Draw lines connecting notes and rests of the same value.

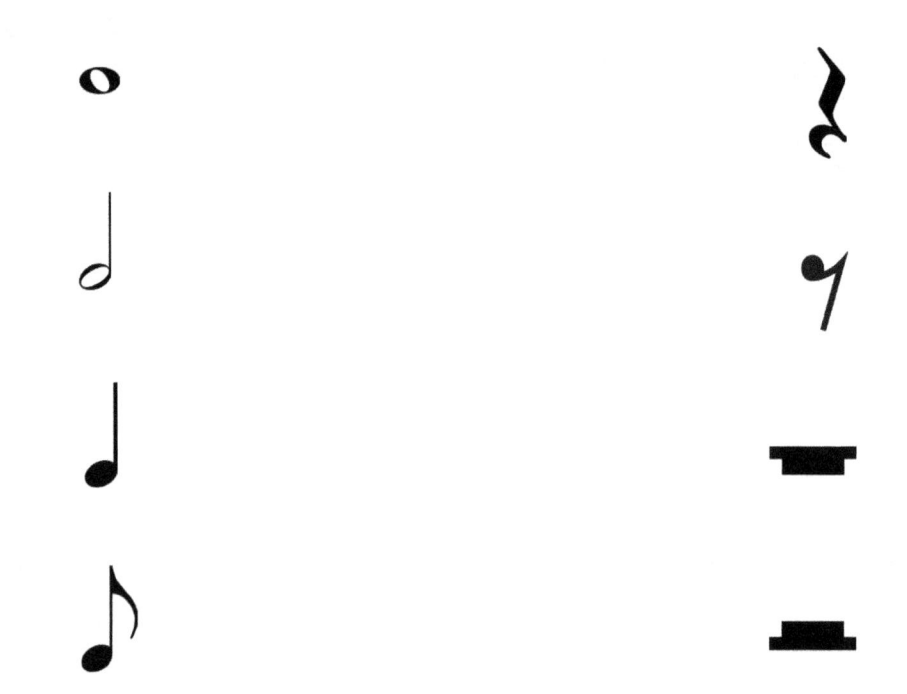

6. Write the names of the following notes and rests.

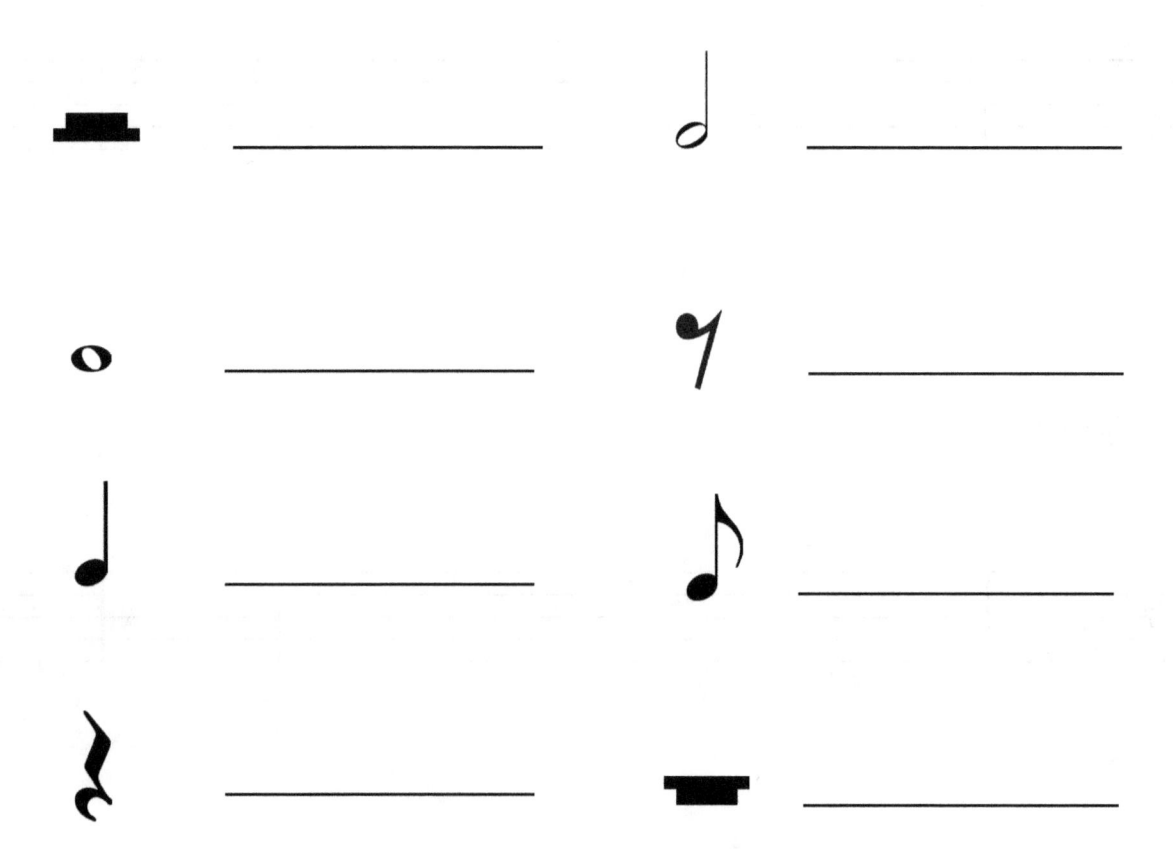

7. Write the following notes and rests in the boxes below.

eighth rest	quarter note	half note
quarter rest	whole rest	eighth note
half rest	whole note	dotted half note

8. Write the number of beats that each rest receives.

9. Fill in the blanks in these sentences.

    (a) A quarter rest receives _____ beat.

    (b) A whole rest receives _____ beats.

    (c) A half rest receives _____ beats.

    (d) An eighth rest receives _____ beats

    (e) A dotted half note receives _____ beats.

    (f) Two eighth notes receive _____ beat.

10. Choose the correct note from the list to complete each equation.

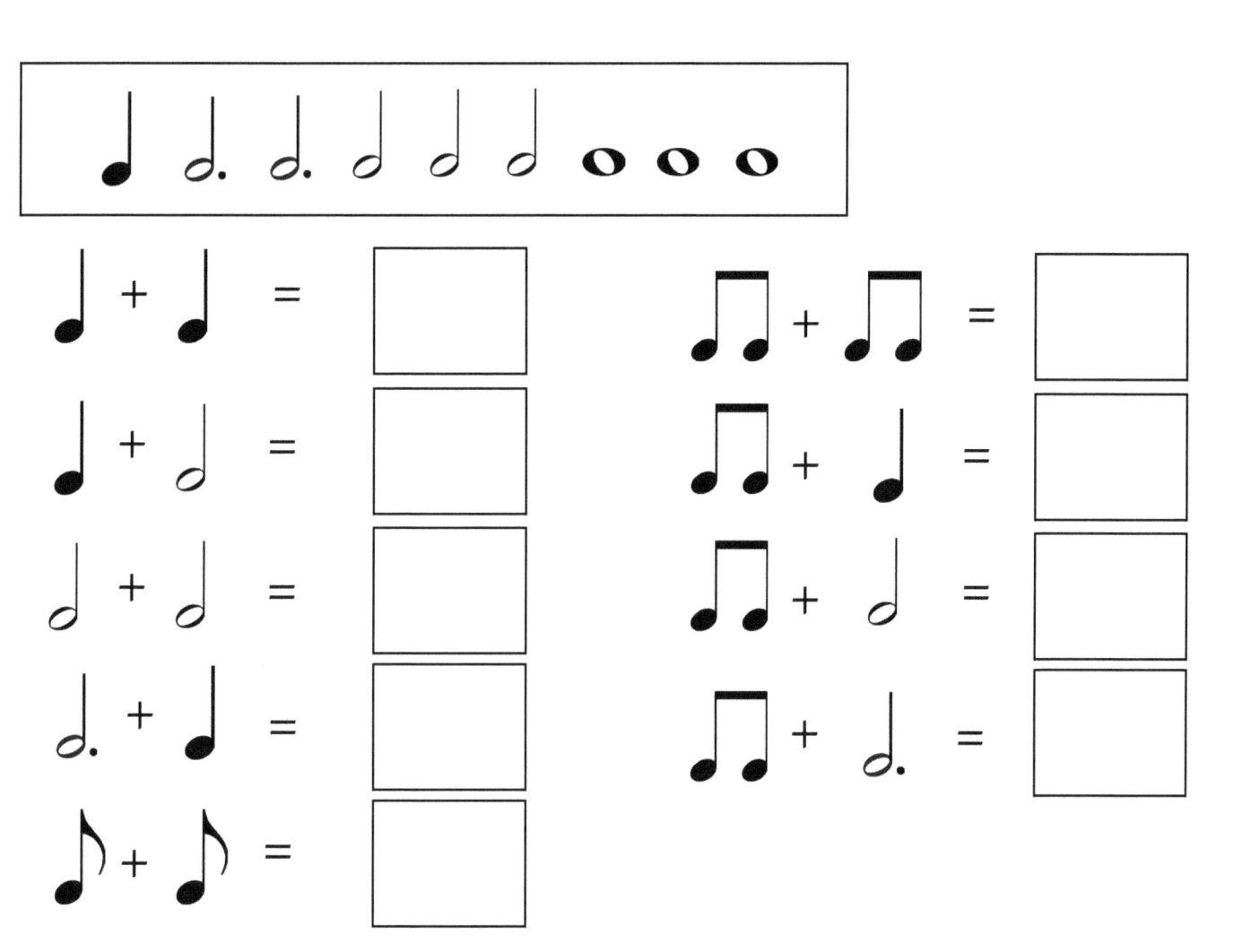

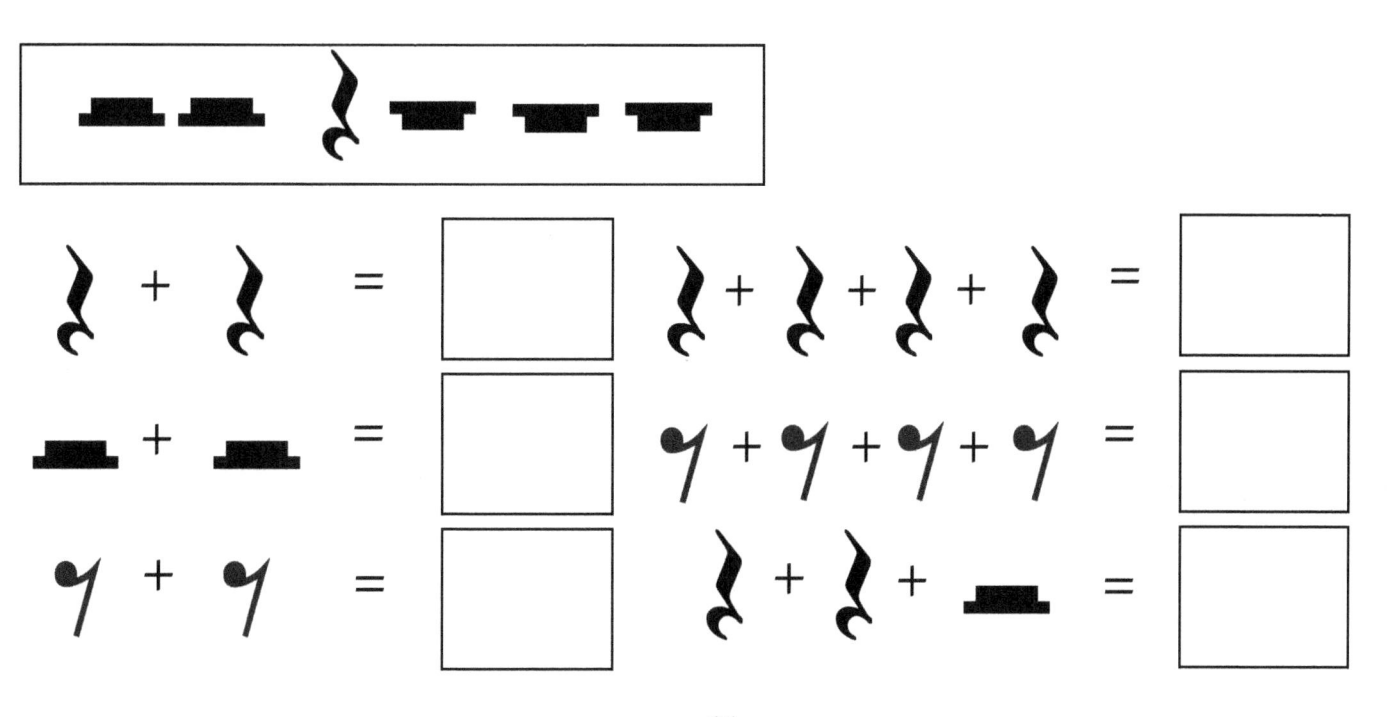

Review Quiz

1. Name these notes.

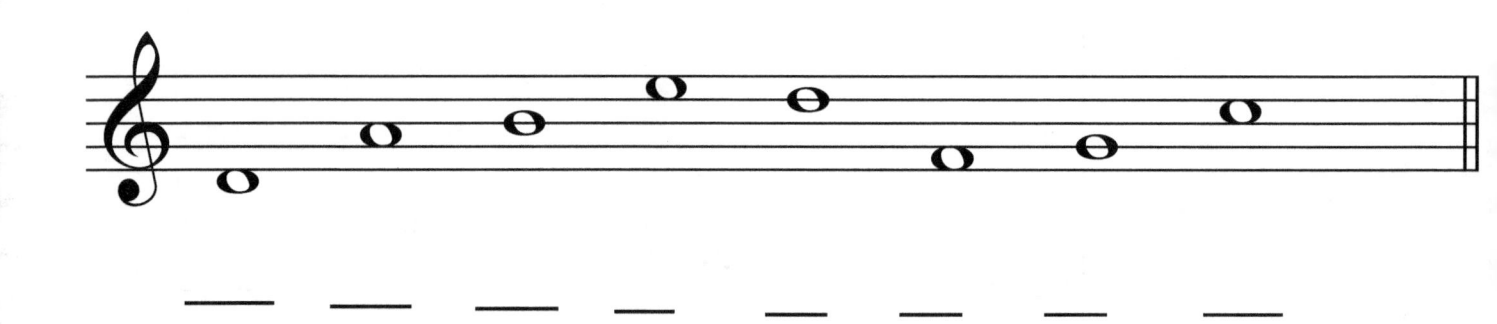

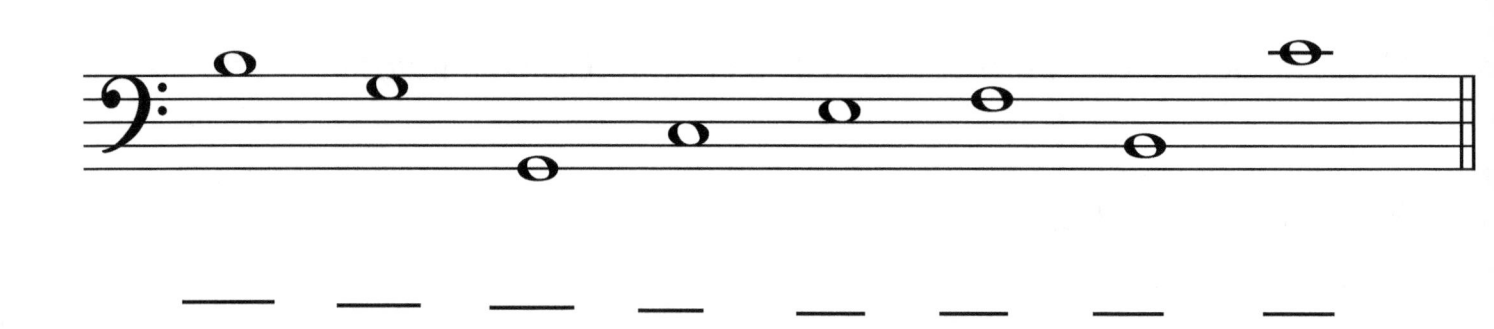

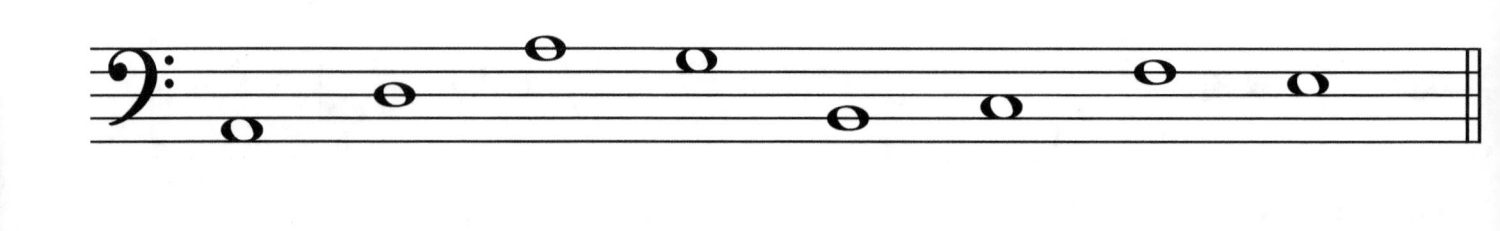

2. Write these notes. Use both lines and spaces.

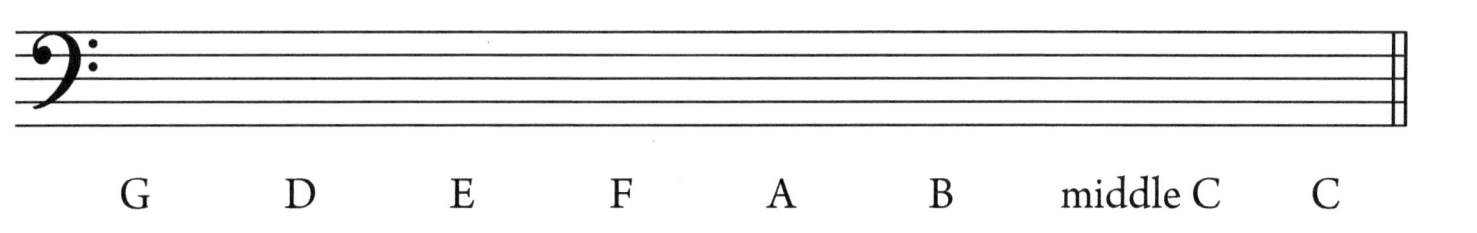

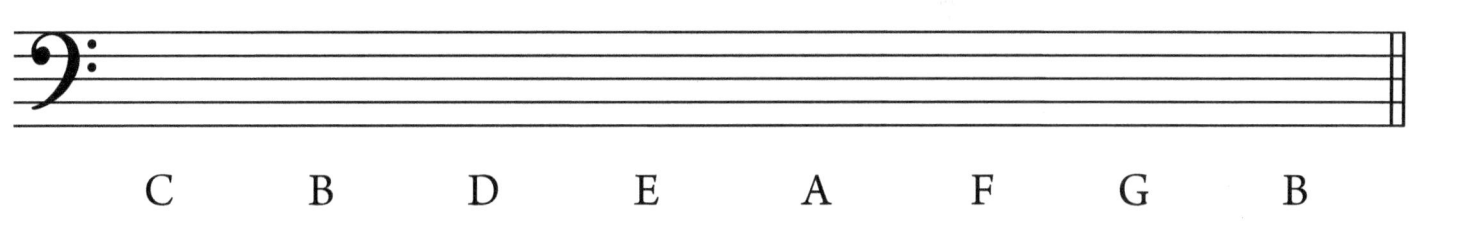

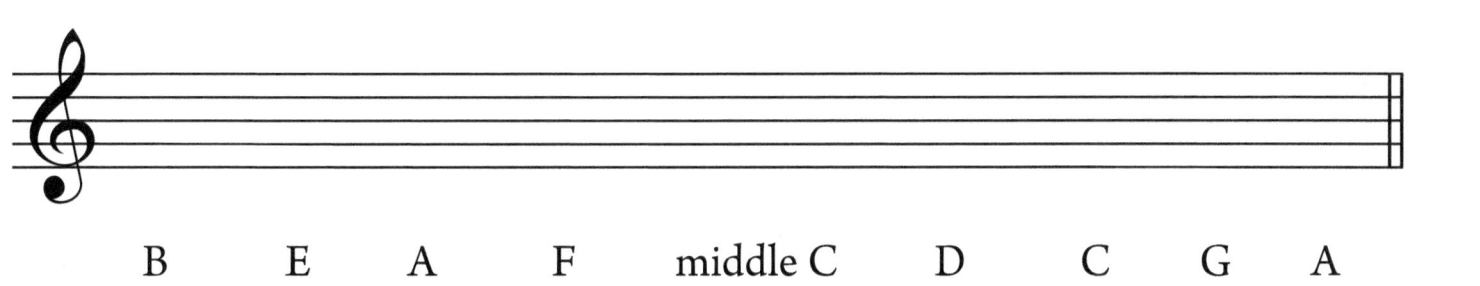

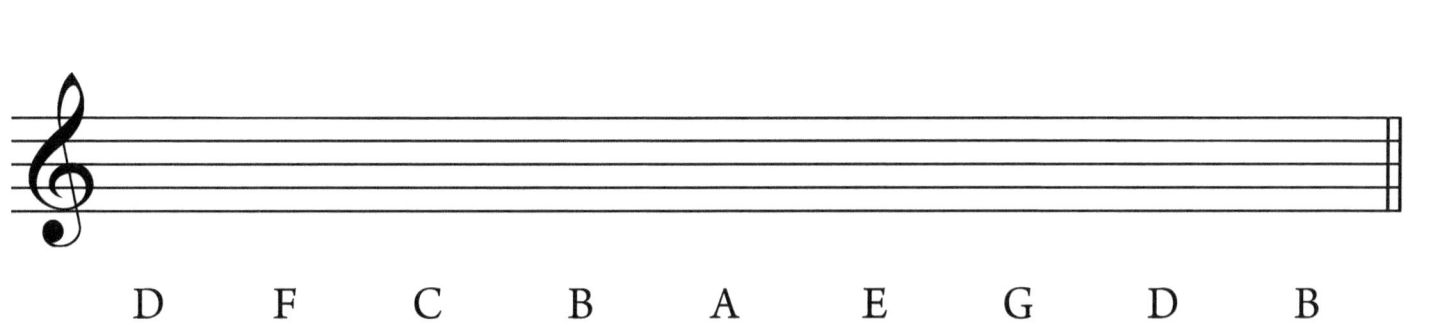

𝄢

    G   D   E   F   A   B   middle C   C

𝄢

    C   B   D   E   A   F   G   B

𝄞

    B   E   A   F   middle C   D   C   G   A

𝄞

    D   F   C   B   A   E   G   D   B

3. Write the signs and the meanings for the following terms.

Term	Sign	Meaning
piano	_____	_____
forte	_____	_____
ritardando	_____	_____
mezzo piano	_____	_____
staccato	_____	_____
mezzo forte	_____	_____
fermata	_____	_____
diminuendo	_____	_____
crescendo	_____	_____

4. Write the number of beats that each note receives.

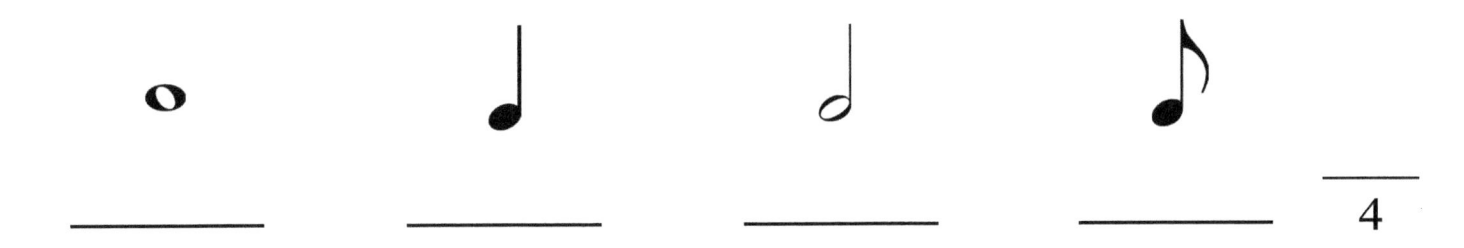

    𝅝   ♩   𝅗𝅥   ♪

_____   _____   _____   _____   4

5. Write the number of beats that each rest receives.

_____   _____   _____   _____   4

6. Write the following notes and rests.

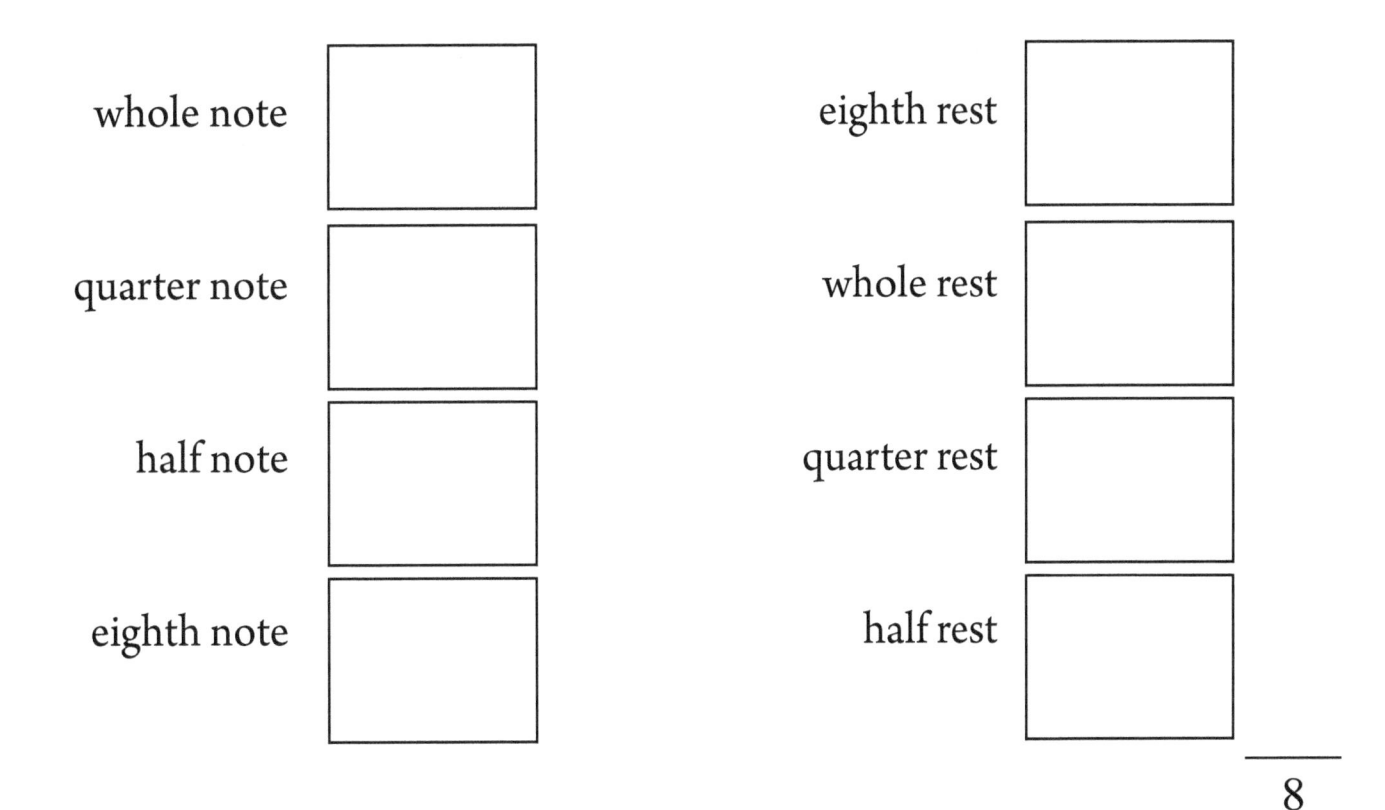

whole note		eighth rest	
quarter note		whole rest	
half note		quarter rest	
eighth note		half rest	

                                                                                                                                                                           8

Congratulations! You're ready for Book 2!

Certificate of Achievement

CONGRATULATIONS TO

_____

You have completed
ELEMENTARY MUSIC THEORY BOOK 1

You are now ready for Elementary Music Theory Book 2

1

Teacher_____

Date_____